HISTORIC
SHIPWRECKS
— OF —
COASTSIDE
CALIFORNIA

JOANN SEMONES

THE
History
PRESS

Published by The History Press
Charleston, SC
www.historypress.com

Front cover: The wreck of the *Roderick Dhu*. *Pacific Grove Museum of Natural History*.

Back cover: Captain Robert "Bully" Waterman. *Mariners' Museum*; the *Point Arena* in heavy seas. *Kelley House Museum*.

First published 2024

Manufactured in the United States

ISBN 9781467155557

Library of Congress Control Number: 2023945942

Notice: The information in this book is true and complete to the best of our knowledge. It is offered without guarantee on the part of the author or The History Press. The author and The History Press disclaim all liability in connection with the use of this book.

To Julie Barrow,
who sails with me through the mystery of history

CONTENTS

INTRODUCTION

S hip disasters come in many forms. They include founderings, groundings and total wrecks. They may happen when a vessel is under her own power or being towed by another ship. They are caused by fog, rain, sleet, heavy seas, unpredictable currents, rocks, reefs, fires, leaks, explosions, collisions with other vessels, foolish miscalculations and simple human error. Whatever the mind can envision, it can happen at sea.

More than twenty years of research is represented in this unique book about selected shipwrecks covering the California Coastside. Told here is the true and full story of each ship and shipwreck, her passengers, officers, crews and even a special mascot.

The key maritime areas contained in this volume are located south of San Francisco along California's central Coastside. They include the geographic regions of Point Montara, Pigeon Point, Año Nuevo, Santa Cruz, Point Pinos and Point Sur. Between 1855 and 1890, lighthouses were built at each crucial site to improve aids to maritime navigation. Shipwrecks both before and after the lighthouses were built are covered.

The shipwrecks within these pages range from the 1850s to the 1950s. They illustrate crafts of all types: clipper ships, barks, schooners, steamers and even experimental vessels. They represent periods ranging from the Age of Sail to the California Gold Rush to the Prohibition era to the Cold War years. Over time, the ships considered here continue to be the most unusual and consequential maritime mishaps along the Coastside.

Some wrecks had devastating losses of life, while some had innovative rescue operations or salvage solutions. Significant artifacts were recovered from other wrecks. One wreck site even became a cemetery that still exists today. The ships taken into account are the *Carrier Pigeon* in 1853, the *Sir John Franklin* in 1865, the *Rydal Hall* in 1876, the *Alice Buck* in 1881, the *Los Angeles* in 1894, the *New York* in 1898, the *City of Florence* in 1900, the *Roderick Dhu* in 1909, the USS *H-3* in 1915, the *Babinda* in 1923, the *San Juan* in 1929, the *CG-256* in 1933, the USS *Macon* in 1935 and the *BARC 1* in 1953.

A notable amount of research time was spent collecting and conducting oral histories of people associated with events that unfolded around each harrowing shipwreck. Therefore, much of this book focuses on human stories—people lost at sea, people facing life-threatening situations and people finding their place in history.

We are reminded that personal reflections and experiences can often offer the most unforgettable insights into our remarkable maritime lore. The poignancy of the human tales offered here is what sets this book apart from others. It is a voyage worth sharing.

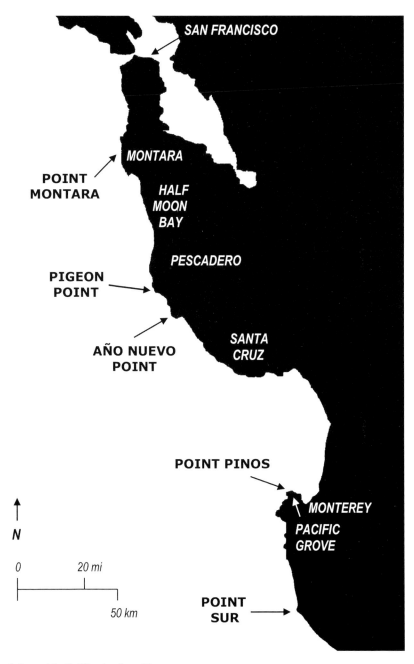

Map of Coastside California. *Janet Taggart.*

Chapter 1

A LASTING LEGACY

Carrier Pigeon, June 6, 1853

S he made only a single voyage, yet she left an enduring legacy. The *Carrier Pigeon* is remembered as one of the finest clipper ships of her day. The point where she foundered on June 6, 1853, is a lasting tribute to her memory and to an era we will never see again.

City of Ships

The period from the 1840s to the 1860s is referred to often as the Golden Age of Sail. The era began in 1843 as a result of the growing demand for more rapid delivery of tea from China and continued under the provocative influence of the discovery of gold in California and Australia in 1848 and 1851. It ended in 1869 when the transcontinental railroad was completed. Linking the eastern United States with California on the Pacific coast, the railway network revolutionized America's transportation system.

During this period, magnificent clipper ships, like the *Carrier Pigeon*, dotted the seas. "Clipper," an American term for a fast sailing vessel, was first applied to speedy schooners and brigs developed at Baltimore for use as privateers, pilot boats and fast transports. It was said that clippers went after the wind rather than waiting for the wind to come to them.

These "greyhounds of the sea" could deliver mail, passengers and manufactured goods at record speeds between the East and West Coasts. From the beginning of the great gold rush to the opening of cross-country

The clipper ship *Carrier Pigeon* was built at Bath, Maine, in 1852. Bath produced the most durable and elegant ships to ever sail. *Colby College.*

rail service, nearly all commerce between the Pacific and Atlantic Oceans was conducted by these swift ships.

Built at Bath, Maine, in 1852 by Trufant, Drummond & Company, the *Carrier Pigeon* was a sleek square-rigged vessel with a knifelike bow, narrow mid-body and deep, straight keel. She was 175 feet long, had a beam of 34 feet and measured 843 tons. Gilbert C. Trufant and the brothers James and William Drummond were partners in the enterprise, which began operating around 1846. According to historian Arthur Rowe, they were "well-known mariners and their ships rendered a good account of themselves."

Bath is commonly known as the "City of Ships." The town sits on the shores of the Kennebec River, about fifteen miles from the Gulf of Maine and forty miles up the coast from Portland. Though compact in population, Bath's impact on Maine, the rest of the United States and even on the world has been anything but small.

During Bath's early days, it built large, wooden yachts and schooners mostly for trade. It was not until 1760 that shipbuilding became an industry in Bath. The growth of shipyards was aided by the nearby abundance of suitable land and wood. The sandy bottom of the river provided good holding for anchorage, along with the absence of any cliffs or rocky outcroppings.

As the hub of American shipping, Bath produced some of the most durable and elegant ships to ever sail. By the mid-nineteenth century, Bath was the nation's fifth-largest seaport, creating clipper ships that sailed to ports around the globe. Production of these quick, hardy, dependable vessels soared. Roughly five thousand ships were launched in the area, which at one time boasted more than two hundred shipbuilding firms.

"Along the Maine Coast, people are born with salt in their blood," author William H. Rowe asserted. "At Bath the stocks producing great ships that carried cargos to the ends of the earth crowded one upon the next along the shore. More ships have been built on that strip of Bath shore front than any other of equal area in the world."

BEST MODELED CLIPPER SHIP

When the *Carrier Pigeon* sailed from Boston in 1853, she was hailed by local newspapers as "the best modeled clipper ship that has gone out of Kennebec this season, built and finished in the best manner." She also boasted a hand-carved gilded figurehead of a pigeon in flight fixed just beneath her bowsprit. Symbolizing the legendary and hallowed history of the message-bearing carrier pigeon, the golden winged bird was meant to inspire the crew. The carrier pigeon was an omen of good luck—fast, dependable, ever returning.

The *Carrier Pigeon*, carrying 1,300 tons of general merchandise, was 130 days out of Boston when she was thrown off course. Having rounded Cape Horn at the tip of South America, she had completed a voyage of more than fifteen thousand miles. The trip around "Cape Stiff," as sailors called it, was not an easy one. "Sudden squalls of winds and fog called willewaks dash with violence over the high lands," one mariner observed, "and in a few minutes shut the scene from view."

Cape Horn's mountainous waves and one-hundred-mile-per-hour gales tested the stamina of even the hardiest ship and crew. This account by an experienced seaman sums up the average experience of rounding the Horn: "The gales such as we have met are not mere gusts or squalls, but long, loud, fierce blasts bearing down on the sea and the ship for hours and hours. The ship mounts huge swells, then plunges into an abyss of foaming water."

Yet challenges along Pacific shores were equally fierce. With its rocky outcroppings, heavy surf, strong currents and thick fog banks, California's coast was one of the most notoriously treacherous in the world. Mariners knew the hazards well. Thick haze lingered persistently, obscuring familiar landmarks and concealing ships at sea. Engulfed in the dense "pea soup" fog common along these shores, navigational readings were often unreliable.

Originally, Pigeon Point was known as Whale Point. In the 1600s, Spanish mariners began charting the area and named it "Punta de las Balenas." The site adjoins Año Nuevo, sharing geographic borders that were established under a land grant in 1842. Called Rancho Punta del Año Nuevo, the tract consisted of seventeen thousand prime acres along San Mateo County shores and included the land at Whale Point.

Unruly currents, brutal waves and tempestuous winds stirred the region's deep moody waters. Jagged reefs lurked beneath the surface. Even knowing this, the *Carrier Pigeon* could not have foreseen her fate. On June 6, 1853, lost in heavy fog and besieged by strong northwest winds, the *Carrier Pigeon* was dangerously off course. The wandering clipper came to grief on a craggy outcropping of rocks not far from her final destination.

Fifteen minutes after the vessel struck, seven feet of water were in the hold. In half an hour, water was above the lower deck. "Her bow lay about 500 feet from the beach," reports said, "and she rests amidships on a ledge of rocks which have broken the ship's back. The tide ebbs and flows in her." The *Carrier Pigeon*'s maiden voyage from Boston to San Francisco ended in calamity. Mercifully, the crew was rescued, but the hapless vessel became the focus of contentious salvage disputes and further disaster.

WRECK ASHORE

To settlers in the isolated coastal village of Pescadero, a three-masted sailing vessel stranded just yards from shore was a novel sight. It was also a unique opportunity to appropriate ship's booty. Crying "Wreck ashore!" curiosity seekers and plunderers alike swarmed the beach. Some offered help to the crew. Others, bobbing about the surf in small rowboats, stripped copper from the ship's hull and carried away valuable cargo.

Many camped on the bluffs nearby, feasting on food from the ship's larder. "There was an abundance of much that was good to eat and drink. Long handled shovels were excellent frying pans," a local scavenger mused. "The menu, though of no great variety, was a surprise—bacon, ham, fresh eggs brought round the Horn in lime water, beans, coffee, hard tack, sweet cakes and preserves in unlimited quantity."

On June 8, the steamer *Active* was dispatched to salvage *Carrier Pigeon*'s payload. The *Active* was diverted to the scene while en route to the Farallon Islands, sixty miles northwest of the wreck site, with the U.S. marshal to remove squatters who laid claim to the area's property.

It was common practice, and maritime law decreed, that the first salvage ship or "wrecker" to reach a stranded vessel could claim the cargo and sell it at auction for the ship owner. Wreckers received a portion of the profits from the sale or were paid a fee by the ship owner. Any delay in recovering cargo meant costly losses for ship owner and wrecker alike.

The *Active*'s good intentions were thwarted by bickering over salvage rights. Apparently, the *Carrier Pigeon*'s captain, Azariah Doane, had misgivings about the *Active*'s recovery operation. "If Captain Doane had not had unfounded fears of salvage claims and had accepted the offered aid of the steamer *Active*," one bystander complained, "he might have saved the new ship and its cargo."

When the *Carrier Pigeon* wrecked in 1853, salvagers swarmed the beach, stripped the ship of valuables and carried away cargo. *From* Harper's New Monthly Magazine.

According to another account, "If the parties interested had allowed *Active* to go to work, without bartering and bantering on salvage, a considerable amount of property might have been saved for the underwriters." The *Active* remained nearby until the arrival of another vessel, the *Sea Bird*.

On June 9, the "ever punctual steamer," *Sea Bird*, arrived. Built at New York in 1850 for the profitable California coastal trade, the 444-ton side-wheeler came to the the *Carrier Pigeon*'s aid from San Francisco. Unfortunately, within thirty-six hours, the *Sea Bird* met with her own mishap only feet away from the helpless *Carrier Pigeon*.

The *Sea Bird* was lying at anchor astern of *Carrier Pigeon* when heavy swells snapped her anchor chains and then her anchor, pitching her onto the rocks. In minutes, the steamer began filling with water. With decks awash and all hands frantically pumping and bilging, the captain ordered the ship beached to save her from sinking.

"BULLY" ARRIVES

On June 11, Captain Robert H. Waterman, commanding the 333-ton steamer *Goliah*, arrived to bring order to the chaos and save as much cargo as possible. A storied ship master, Captain Waterman had earned the infamous moniker of "Bully" after being charged with brutality on the clipper *Challenge*.

Born in Hudson, New York, in 1808, he was the son of Nantucket whaling captain Thaddeus Waterman. "Hudson is a vibrant town," the *New York Journal* reported. "The city has several fine wharves, four large warehouses, a covered rope-walk, works for producing whale oil and whale bone products, 150 dwelling-houses, shops, barns, one of the best distilleries in America, 1,500 souls and twenty-five seagoing vessels."

After his father died at sea when he was eight, Waterman moved with his mother and three siblings to Fairfield, Connecticut. Waterman first went to sea at age twelve aboard a China trader and spent most of the next nine years aboard transatlantic packet ships (which carried cargo and passengers). Although they were not designed for speed, they were known for departing port on a regular schedule.

By 1829, Waterman had been promoted to first mate of the packet *Britannia*. His captain, Charles H. Marshall, later bought the packet *South America* and made Waterman the skipper. In 1836, Waterman accepted command of the cotton freighter *Natchez*, guiding the ship on several voyages around Cape Horn. In 1842, the *Natchez* shifted to the China trade, and Waterman sailed her to Macao, China. His return trip to New York took only seventy-eight days, a new record.

During the late 1840s, Waterman received command of the clipper *Sea Witch*. According to historian A.B.C. Whipple, Waterman worked with the ship's designer on much of the ship's rig and sail plan, "specifying 140-foot-tall masts and more square footage of sail than a 74-gun warship." In 1847, he brought the *Sea Witch* from Hong Kong to New York in just seventy-seven days.

Throughout his career, Waterman attracted attention for his efficiency and ability to maintain order and discipline among passengers and crew. He even became something of a hero, rescuing a sailor who fell overboard from aloft during a gale.

In 1851, despite expressing his intention to retire from the sea, Waterman took command of the clipper *Challenge*. The shipping company was seeking a high-quality captain for its newest vessel, offering him a $10,000 bonus if he could get the ship to San Francisco within ninety days of departure. Waterman accepted the *Challenge* and took it out of New York on July 13. That very first day, he quarreled with and dismissed the first mate, replacing him with James Douglass, hired off the deck of a packet.

Captain Robert "Bully" Waterman, a storied ship master, brought controversy to the wreck site and may have named Pigeon Point. *Mariners' Museum.*

Unfortunately, the shipping company failed to provide *Challenge* with an experienced crew. The huge demand for sailors occasioned by clippers sailing for the California gold fields had left few competent seamen in New York. Half of the ship's fifty-six-man complement had never sailed, and only three were able seamen. Many were recent immigrants who could speak no English. Discipline, morale and seamanship were predictably poor.

During the trip around Cape Horn, mutiny broke out, and drastic measures were taken to enforce order and obedience. According to local newspapers accounts, when the ship finally arrived in San Francisco, crew members alleged that "five seamen were beaten and kicked to death, four others had been deliberately shaken from the rigging, and five more, mangled and maimed, still lay on the ship." A mob demanded that Waterman be turned over for hanging or burning.

At his own request, Waterman stood trial. He was exonerated and settled in California with his wife, Cordelia. He founded the city of Fairfield in 1856, named after his former home in Connecticut. He raised poultry and cattle and served as San Francisco's port warden and inspector of hulls. Yet the debate continued, even after his death in 1884. To some, he was Captain "Bob," a hard worker and conscientious master. To others, he was "Bully" Waterman, a brute and a murderer.

PIGEON POINT'S NAMESAKE

Controversy over Waterman's reputation hindered the *Goliah*'s rescue effort. "He attempted to enforce upon the boys the overbearing dictum of the experience of his shipmasters' tyrannical manners and mode," one salvager snorted.

Whatever the truth may be, Waterman's salvage terms for the *Carrier Pigeon* were liberal. He wanted all unbroken and uninjured articles and packages. Other wreckers could have everything else. The *Goliah* took the crews from the *Carrier Pigeon* and the *Sea Bird* to San Francisco and then returned to remove freight and machinery from both ships.

The *Carrier Pigeon*, with cargo and freight, was insured for $195,000, with the ship being valued at $54,000. However, the wreck and cargo "were sold as they lay" for $1,500. Most of the cargo between decks, part of it damaged, was recovered. Ultimately, more than 1,200 packages of merchandise were saved.

Flung across the jagged rocks, the *Carrier Pigeon* and the *Sea Bird* lay like forlorn gulls with broken wings. According to one report, "Much expense was incurred and many fruitless efforts were made to float the *Sea Bird*. It was at last accomplished by means of long iron cylinders made for the purpose and placed under the vessel."

Over the next six months, the *Sea Bird* was conveyed to port and repaired. She resumed her coastal transport, "performing years of good service for her owners." In 1857, the little ship survived a massive tidal wave caused by an earthquake, only to burn at the water line off Discovery Island, Canada, one year later.

The *Carrier Pigeon* was even less fortunate. According to the underwriters' notice, "The ship then being full of water, her back broken, is momentarily expected to go to pieces, being exposed to the full force of the surf which beat over her." Within days, the once graceful clipper ship splintered and sank slowly from sight.

Some said that the vessel was so beaten by the roaring surf that a piece of the ship's gilded figurehead washed ashore. If so, its whereabouts are unknown. The *Carrier Pigeon*'s only remnant is the ship's bell, now in the hands of a private collector.

The incident was so unforgettable that two versions exist regarding the naming of the site where the *Carrier Pigeon* wrecked. According to one story, when the next shipload of locally grown potatoes reached San Francisco, someone reported that it was arriving from Carrier Pigeon Point. Before long, the name was shortened to Pigeon Point.

The other account insists that the point was named by Captain Waterman and an unknown resident. According to this story, in sending a letter to his principals in San Francisco, Waterman inquired about the site's identity. "I told him it had none but said it was in the neighborhood of New Year's Point," the resident recalled.

"To this he objected and proposed dating his letter from Carrier Pigeon Point. Deeming this title good enough but somewhat lengthy, I proposed he drop the Carrier and call the point Pigeon Point," the man continued. "This satisfied the captain and it was so named."

In either case, it was through the *Carrier Pigeon*'s misfortune that she gained immortality.

CHAPTER 2

ALL WAS TERROR AND CONFUSION

SIR JOHN FRANKLIN, JANUARY 17, 1865

Bold, adventurous and ill-fated, the *Sir John Franklin* collided with destiny on January 17, 1865. All that remains is a near-forgotten cemetery between Pigeon Point and Año Nuevo, a poignant reminder of the dangers of the sea.

BEAUTIFUL LAUNCH

On an icy December day in 1853, the elegant ship *Sir John Franklin* was launched a little before four o'clock in the afternoon. "She went overboard in most beautiful style. A more easy, regular and beautiful launch we never witnessed," the *Baltimore Sun* reported. "While standing upon the wharf, amid a driving snow storm, we were involuntarily led to think that a more proper time could not have been chosen for launching a vessel named after a navigator, who, in all probability, has perished among the snows and ice of the northern regions."

Like the famed British Arctic explorer whose name the ship bore, the *Sir John Franklin* was destined for her fair share of adventure. The 171-foot vessel was completed at Baltimore, Maryland, in 1854 by John J. Abrams & Sons. Between 1841 and 1867, Abrams was a well-known shipbuilder in the Fells Point District, a large, bustling waterfront filled with maritime trades and shipping operations. With an abundance of native timber and iron ore for building ships, as well as hemp and flax for producing sails and cordage, Baltimore grew early and rapidly into an important seaport.

The clipper ship *Sir John Franklin* was built at Baltimore, Maryland, in 1854. Initially, she served in the Mankin Line of packet ships. *Mariners' Museum.*

The clipper served first as one of the Mankin Line packets. In the early 1840s, there were no regular shipping lines between Baltimore, Maryland, and Liverpool, England. Vessels came and went in a random manner with no routine sailing dates. In 1848, Henry Mankin established a regular line of ships adapted to passenger as well as to freight traffic.

Henry Mankin was born 1804 in Baltimore, Maryland, and his childhood and youth were spent at his father's country homes. His mother's early death, before he was nine years old, affected him deeply. He was sent to school to Dr. Gray, a noted educator of the time, and was happy with the special interest shown in him. Later, faced with financial difficulties, his father placed him in his counting house.

The young man grew delighted in ships and mercantile problems and eagerly threw himself into what would become his life's work. Later, he entered the house of Clark & Kellogg, a prominent firm in Baltimore. He was promoted to manager, then partner, taking over the business when the two partners retired. According to a biographer, "His energy and enterprise were now fully shown. His ships were sent to ports throughout Europe and Asia, taking cargo into one port and discharging it at another far away where it was needed."

Liverpool Packet

Mankin is best known for developing the "Liverpool packets," which prospered for twenty years. Demand for North American timber and cotton as raw materials for British industry led to an established transatlantic trade. Immigrants from the British Isles and mainland Europe, along with British manufactured goods, provided a useful return cargo.

"Each vessel brought several hundred immigrants who were distributed along the street in groups awaiting wagons to convey them to the railroad stations," reported the *Baltimore Sun*. "It was a pleasure for Mr. Mankin that he was enabling strong, healthy men and women to find good homes in this country where their work was needed."

The *Sir John Franklin* and other ships involved in the demanding packet trade made regular transatlantic voyages year round. Depending on the time of year, passages could be as fast as twenty days or as slow as fifty or more outbound from Baltimore. The journey back from Liverpool could be even longer, and no doubt more trying, during winter months. No matter how light or heavy the cargo, human or otherwise, the Liverpool packets maintained their schedules and became one of the mainstays of the sailing industry.

In the 1860s, steam started to replace sail on the transatlantic route. With the loss of the packet market in sight, Mankin sought broader opportunities. The *Sir John Franklin* was pressed into service to meet more promising commercial needs on the Pacific coast.

On the first leg of her final journey to San Francisco, the *Sir John Franklin* stopped in Rio de Janeiro. There the clipper took on unexpected cargo from the *Charles L. Pennell*. Bound for San Francisco from New York, the *Charles L. Pennell* put into port in distress and was subsequently condemned. The combined cargo of dry goods, lumber, pianos and three hundred barrels of spirits carried by the *Sir John Franklin* was insured for $350,000.

Along with the surplus cargo, Captain John Despeau took on an extra hand, Robert Dawson Owens, a supercargo. Typically, the supercargo was a seaman wishing to exchange work for free passage to another port. In this instance, Owens was a representative of the firm handling the sale and disposition of goods from the *Charles L. Pennell*.

The *Sir John Franklin* carried nineteen other crew, including seamen Edward J. Church, John Devine, Charles Martin, John Sooltine and Jacob Staten. Church was only sixteen years old.

"IT WASN'T NO CASTLE"

Ordinary seamen like Edward Church were extraordinary souls, for a sailor's life during the era of sail was exceptionally harsh. He faced danger, deprivation and a daily grind of rigorous labor. Yet he eagerly went to sea. Usually, a boy apprenticed himself at about age twelve, serving two or three years before becoming an ordinary seaman. The next step up the ladder was able-bodied seaman. Annual pay rates for able seamen were around eighteen dollars per month, for ordinary seamen twelve dollars and as little as eight dollars for boys.

Sailors could be assigned to specific jobs on board such as a cook, surgeon or carpenter. A boatswain was in charge of the sails. A quartermaster was the helmsman and performed ship control, navigation and bridge watch duties. Other members of the crew would, of course, carry out all the duties, including keeping watch, handling sails and cleaning decks. They might spend their limited off-duty hours playing games of dice and cards, telling tales, playing musical instruments, carving, drawing, making models or practicing knots.

Even on "a first class ship" such as the *Sir John Franklin*, the living environment was miserably cramped. At her broadest point, the clipper was only thirty-six feet wide. Since most of the 999-ton vessel carried precious cargo, a seaman's quarters were confined to the forecastle, or "fo'c'sle." In this meager space, he slept on a tiny slatted bunk with barely enough room for clothes and keepsakes from home. "It wasn't no castle," one old salt proclaimed.

The crew on sailing ships typically owned little property. A sailor might own a small sea chest, sometimes called a "ditty box." It would have been one of his most important possessions. Not only did the chest store a sailor's personal belongings and mementos, but it also served as his table, chair, bank and bureau. These chests also gave a sailor an opportunity for personal expression through carvings, paintings and decorations.

A variety of victuals might be eaten for breakfast, lunch or dinner, including salt pork or salt beef, bean soup, boiled rice, bread with molasses, coffee and always plenty of seabiscuit or hard tack. Other concoctions were scouse, a beef hash mixed with potatoes or biscuits, and pease, a dried portable soup regarded as an acceptable substitute for fresh vegetables. Along with the usual ration of grog, a flour pudding called duff was savored in the evening.

During the voyage, Church and each of his mates were expected to stand as helmsman steering the ship. Another primary duty was reefing, or

A sailor's life during the era of sail was exceptionally harsh. He faced danger, deprivation and a daily grind of rigorous labor. *Mariners' Museum.*

shortening sails by ropes called reef lines, to reduce the area of sail exposed to the wind. All mariners agreed that "competent knowledge of steering, reefing and furling makes a sailor."

By far, the most hazardous job was furling, for it meant taking in sail when the weather was at its worst. Seamen scrambled up into wet, swaying rigging and out onto slippery yards to gather up billowing canvas, punch it into shape and lash it down. On a ship like the *Sir John Franklin*, which carried more sail than most other clippers of the day, the task was especially dangerous.

In addition to these death-defying activities, Church and his shipmates faced other perils. Physical injuries were all too common. Maladies such as dysentery, consumption, pleurisy, anemia and scurvy were constant threats. "A sailor's life at best is a mixture of a little good with much evil," author Richard Henry Dana revealed, "and a little pleasure with much pain."

And then there was always the risk of shipwreck.

Far Out to Sea

On the misty evening of January 17, 1865, fearing that the *Sir John Franklin* was entering breakers, First Officer Boyd roused Captain Despeau from his sleep. Due to thick fog, readings hadn't been taken for more than twenty-four hours. Yet according to the captain's reckoning, the vessel was "far out to sea." Believing his ship to be seventy miles from shore, Captain Despeau had headed inland unwittingly.

From the deck came the lookout's cry, "Breakers ahead!" Immediately, Captain Despeau gave the order to "wear ship." A dangerous maneuver, he was attempting to run with the wind by quickly turning the vessel in a sharp U-turn. Desperately, the clipper fought to gain open water, but the fury of the sea proved overwhelming. The misguided vessel crashed against the rocks brutally. The first blow punctured a huge hole in the hull. The second and third strikes broke the defenseless ship in half, spilling cargo and crew into the treacherous surf.

"She struck with great violence on the rocks, staving her bottom, and carrying her masts overboard," First Officer Boyd stated later. "In a few minutes, the vessel parted amidships and all was terror and confusion."

After two grueling hours of struggling in dark, frigid water, First Officer Boyd, Second Officer Ball, Third Officer Welch and five unnamed seamen gained the shore. Sadly, the strong undertow carried Captain Despeau,

Seaman Church and the rest of the crew out to sea. "This is the second ship lost at the same point," local newspapers declared later, "and is by far the most disastrous shipwreck which has ever happened on our coast."

Wet, cold and exhausted, survivors wandered the shore for several more hours before reaching the safety of a farmhouse. "They were hospitably cared for, every attention being paid to them," a resident disclosed. "In the morning the neighbors came to bring relief with clothing, and kindly furnished Mr. Boyd with means of conveyance to the city."

Hoping to salvage some of the cargo, the *Sir John Franklin*'s owners dispatched a sheriff and six policemen to the scene. "Everything is a confused mass of boxes and barrels," newspapers observed. "Hundreds of men are gathering in the floating packages of clothes, liquors and pianos, all in damaged condition save the barreled liquids."

Sharp-eyed beachcombers also picnicked on tins of turkey, chicken, oysters and fruit found embedded in the sand. If driftwood was too wet, fires were easily made from cans of coal oil bobbing in the surf. Occasionally, sharp explosions echoed from the beach—merely novices who'd forgotten to punch a hole in the can before warming it in the fire.

Curiously, dozens of the three hundred barrels of spirits listed on the ship's manifest disappeared. Eventually, two hundred casks of whiskey were recovered and later sold in San Francisco. Some eager buyers complained that their kegs had been tampered with and refilled with saltwater. Apparently, many had been drained by thirsty Coastside residents.

Remembered Still

The *Sir John Franklin*'s salt-scoured quarterboard, or nameplate, washed ashore and was saved by a local farmer. For nearly a century, the souvenir hung in a barn. Today, it is part of the archives of the San Francisco Maritime National Historical Park.

The bodies of two officers and four seamen were recovered also. In life, although the crew of the *Sir John Franklin* hailed from different parts of the globe, they all recognized the ranking system of a ship at sea. In death, accordingly, they were buried based on that status.

Captain John Despeau of Baltimore and supercargo Robert Dawson Owens of New York were taken to San Francisco and buried at Lone Mountain Cemetery. Years later, the cemetery was abandoned. Unfortunately, many of the bodies were deposited in a mass grave at Cypress Lawn Cemetery.

After the *Sir John Franklin* foundered, a stone monument was created. One of the crew was just sixteen years old. *San Mateo County History Museum.*

Seamen John Devine of England, Charles Martin of Norway and John Sooltine and Jacob Staten, both of Finland, were buried on a sandy bluff near the site of the wreck. Mrs. Church was so overcome by the loss of her son, Edward, that she commissioned the placement of a marble tombstone in his memory. The monument remained until it was stolen in the late 1960s. The site, now known as Franklin Point, is part of Año Nuevo State Park.

Over the years, strong winds eroded sand dunes covering the graves. In 1980, an unsuspecting hiker discovered exposed human remains. Archaeological work in the area uncovered four redwood coffins two years later. Most likely, they are the coffins of the four seamen buried at the point after the wreck of the *Sir John Franklin*. Their bones have since been reinterred and rest protected from further intrusion.

Between 1983 and 2001, the skeletal remains of eight individuals were recovered. Evidently, passengers from two other shipwrecks in the 1860s were also hastily buried at the point. According to a state archaeologist, "Historic accounts describe how local residents rallied to recover the dead that had washed up on the beach and worked to bury them in redwood caskets in dune fields out on the narrow point that has ever since been named after the wreck of the *Sir John Franklin*."

Today, two large deck areas serve as protective barriers over the reburial location. It is also a place where people can linger to contemplate the historic site and its magnificent maritime views. Though shrouded by the sands of time, the crew of the *Sir John Franklin*, as well as their toil and sacrifice, is remembered still.

CHAPTER 3

A TERRIBLE NIGHT

RYDAL HALL, OCTOBER 17, 1876

The three-masted British vessel *Rydal Hall* crashed in the vicinity of Point Montara on October 17, 1876. The ship, the cargo and ten of the ship's panic-stricken crew perished. Portions of the ship's sunken hulk were discovered nearly one hundred years later.

CARDIFF COAL

In the otherwise pastoral valleys of South Wales, it was the iron industry that caused the tiny town of Cardiff to evolve as a port. Initially, the demand for iron was fueled by the Royal Navy, which needed cannons for its ships, and later by the construction of new railroad systems.

In 1794, a canal was completed linking Cardiff with Merthyr. Located just north of Cardiff, Merthyr was situated close to vast reserves of iron ore, coal, limestone and water, making it an ideal site for ironworks. In 1798, a basin was created, connecting the canal to the sea. Cardiff's first dock was built in 1839, and two years later a railway was opened, igniting the city's growth.

"The inhabitants of this town carry on considerable trade and send thither great quantities of oats, barley, salt butter and poultry of all kinds," a writer noted. "There are not less than 8,780 tons of cast iron and wrought iron shipped annually to London and other places."

In the 1850s, coal quickly replaced iron as the industrial foundation of South Wales. A reliable energy source for hundreds of years, coal was an important fuel for cities, industries, railroads and steamships. With yearly exports reaching 2 million tons as early as 1862, Cardiff coal was what oil is today.

Originally, coal was brought down from the hills and valleys on the backs of mules. Their burden was laid down at a small quay, where vessels of small tonnage awaited to carry the cargo to other ports. By 1870, with its burgeoning docks and railways, Cardiff was providing 30 percent of Britain's coal exports. "The scene on the wharves is very stirring," an observer wrote. "There is a network of railways about the docks, giving direct communication to every port in the kingdom."

FAT CARGO CARRIER

Ships like the *Rydal Hall* were used as colliers to transport coal from Cardiff to British ports as well as ports around the world. The *Rydal Hall* was constructed in 1874 at Liverpool, England, by the highly respected R. & J. Evans Company. The firm, which advertised itself as "shipbuilders, repairers and boiler makers," continued building fine iron sailing ships into the 1890s.

The *Rydal Hall*'s owner was Robert Alexander. Born in Belfast, Ireland, he was a distinguished shipbroker who established the Sun Shipping Company in 1868. With Alexander's penchant for naming his ships "Hall" after notable people and places in Britain, the enterprise was known popularly as the Hall Line. Indeed, it was his hallmark. However, it wasn't until 1899 that the company name was officially changed to Hall Line Ltd.

By 1874, the venture was operating forty ships, mostly steamships, and the company's routes had expanded worldwide. Outward cargoes were primarily coal and manufactured goods. Return cargoes included cotton, jute and spices from India and grain from Australia. The 1,771-ton *Rydal Hall* served as both a cargo and passenger ship, providing service to America, Australia and India.

Soon after setting sail on her maiden voyage from Liverpool to San Francisco, the *Rydal Hall* was caught in a gale off the coast of Cornwall, England. The vessel came dangerously close to the Seven Stones Reef, which rises out of deep water and is a notorious navigational hazard. More than seventy named wrecks and an estimated total of two hundred shipwrecks have occurred in the area. Although the *Rydal Hall* lost much of her rigging

On her maiden voyage from Liverpool to San Francisco in 1875, the *Rydal Hall* nearly wrecked off the coast of Cornwall, England. *National Maritime Museum.*

in the storm, she was located on April 20, 1875, by the paddle tug *Queen of the Bay* and towed to the Isles of Scilly, off the southwestern tip of Cornwall.

Little is recorded about other voyages until 1876. Again bound for San Francisco, the *Rydal Hall* departed Cardiff on June 23 under the command of Captain Henry Foster. More than 260 feet long and 42 feet wide, the iron vessel was hailed by the local press as "a fat cargo carrier which could match anybody else's hulls for capacity." In addition to a crew of thirty-three, she carried 2,551 tons of coal consigned for Balfour, Guthrie & Company.

FIRST-CLASS HOUSE

Balfour, Guthrie & Company was associated with the eminent British firm of Balfour, Williamson & Company. Established by three Scotsmen in 1851, Balfour, Williamson & Company began as a meager merchant shipping and South American trade enterprise and grew into a "first-class Liverpool house."

One writer noted, "Liverpool is a very rich trading town. The houses are of brick and stone, built high and the streets look very handsome. There is an abundance of people who are well dressed and fashionable. It's London in miniature."

Alexander Balfour ran the Liverpool operation, while his two partners, Stephen Williamson and David Duncan, worked in Valparaiso, Chile. After a falling out with Balfour, Duncan left the partnership to begin his own company.

On a voyage to Chile in 1864, Balfour experienced the difficult conditions sailors endured, especially rounding the infamous Cape Horn. "Wet to the skin, the crew spent hours clinging to the yardarms. Because of the danger of fire, no drying facilities or fires were allowed," one account said. "At this point in the journey, fresh food had usually run out. This resulted in many of the crew suffering from poor health that often led to a premature death."

When he returned to Liverpool, Balfour founded the Duke Street Home to provide better conditions for sailors. He was also a founder of orphanages for seamen's children, as well as the Seamen's Institute. When Balfour died in 1886, a monument was erected in his memory on the grounds of St. John's Gardens in Liverpool. The inscription reads, "His life was devoted to God in noble and munificent efforts for the benefit of sailors, the education of people, and the promotion of all good works."

Having acquired considerable experience trading from Chile with large, efficient sailing ships, the trio expanded operations to San Francisco in 1869 by establishing Balfour, Guthrie & Company. Initially, the firm imported British industrial goods and exported wheat from California. It soon established the largest grain export and fruit packing venture in the West. Alexander Balfour's brother, Robert, and Alexander Guthrie were principal officers of the firm.

In 1876, Balfour, Guthrie & Company opened an office in Portland, Oregon, followed by one in Tacoma, Washington, in 1888. Other branches of Balfour, Williamson & Company were established worldwide well into the 1900s.

PANIC-STRICKEN CREW

The *Rydal Hall*'s long journey from Cardiff proved uneventful until the evening of October 17, 1876. Running along with a light breeze and in thick fog, Captain Foster believed his ship to be farther north than he was.

Unable to take readings as the fog thickened, he gave the order to "heave to." This is a way of slowing the ship's forward progress by fixing the helm and foresail position so that the vessel doesn't have to be actively steered. This tactic was commonly used while waiting out a storm or other bad weather.

"As the night wore on it grew thicker and thicker, and we grew a little nervous. All the officers and myself remained on deck and were on deck when she struck," Captain Foster stated later. "I did not hear any fog whistle nor had I any idea where we were. She did not strike hard, but it appeared as if her bottom was crushed and she rapidly filled with water."

Panic-stricken, four of the crew—George Johns, George Geoger, George White and Charles Wilson—seized a small boat without the captain's orders and lowered away. Unluckily, the boat swamped in the heavy surf, and all were drowned.

Moments later, the captain ordered the lifeboat to be cleared away, putting Second Mate Hugh Williams in charge. After considerable confusion, eight men—including Williams; seamen William Baker, Alexander Barlow and James Gomez; steward Fred Davis; and steward's boy William Wilson, along with apprentices C. Clayton and Keith Selwyn—clambered aboard.

As the men struggled to lower the lifeboat, huge waves broke over the deck, flinging the boat overboard. Everyone was catapulted into the churning water. Somehow, Clayton and Davis managed to swim to some rocks and cling to them until being plucked off by a band of courageous local fishermen. Sadly, the others, including Selwyn, who was only sixteen years old, were swallowed by the sea.

Captain Foster made no further attempts to lower the lifeboats. With little hope, he and the remaining crew stayed aboard the sinking ship until morning. Fortunately, vessels from a nearby whaling station arrived and with some difficulty rescued the bedraggled group. "We passed a terrible night on the wrecked ship," the captain declared, "the sea beating over her all night and the cold being almost insufferable."

Toward morning, the tide receded, leaving the ship's decks almost clear. The *Rydal Hall* still hung firm on the rocks about an eighth of a mile from the shore. With her hold full of water and her hull breaking, the vessel's chance of surviving was gone. One observer reflected, "She was a fine iron ship."

GRAVE ERROR

The *Rydal Hall's* wreckage was auctioned by S.L. Jones & Company on October 20 at the Merchants' Exchange in San Francisco. It sold for $850 to commission merchants Breeze and Loughran. "If we have fine weather,"

Divers John Koepf (center) and Roy Lee (right) discovered a cannon and the precious ship's bell from the *Rydal Hall*. *John Koepf.*

newspapers commented, "they will raise a good profit on their investment by saving spars, sails, rigging, anchors, chains and provisions."

Unfortunately, the crippled ship languished on the rocks without a thing being done toward salvage. Apparently, some difficulty occurred between the purchasers and the men they hired to perform recovery efforts. Nothing was salvaged, not even the ship's papers. Valued at $120,000, the vessel and her cargo were a total loss.

Gradually, the *Rydal Hall* began cracking apart. Chunks of Cardiff coal, cabin fittings and other debris spilled into the water and onto the beach. A large portion of the vessel's woodwork was sighted drifting past the Cliff House, a restaurant perched on a high pinnacle on the outskirts of San Francisco.

Local townspeople gathered to scoop up coal washing onto the beach. It would provide free fuel for the coming winter months. Francisco "Chico" Gonzales retrieved something else: a plain wooden sea chest bobbing in the surf. Through the years, the chest was passed on to others in the family.

"That old sea chest has been around since I was a little kid," Chico's great-grandson John E. Gonzales Jr. exclaimed. "My dad packed it around with him everywhere, in the navy and to all the lighthouses where he served." It was an appropriate memento, indeed, for John Sr., who was head keeper at Point Montara Lighthouse from 1955 to 1963.

Meanwhile, Silas Casey Jr., the district lighthouse inspector, investigated Captain Foster's allegation that the fog signal was inaudible. Casey was a respected naval officer and veteran of the Civil War. After graduating from the Annapolis Naval Academy in 1860, he served aboard ships in both the Southern and Northern Blockading Squadrons. By 1876, when he was assigned to the Lighthouse Service, he had risen to the rank of commander.

Commander Casey verified that the whaling crews could hear the whistle distinctly and that on the night of the wreck, the wind had been blowing in a southerly direction. The log of the Point Montara fog station showed that the fog signal was running at an average of seventy pounds per square inch of steam, which meant that it was heard within a radius of three miles. Casey concluded that since the ship went ashore about two and a half miles from Point Montara, the crew had to have heard it.

Casey's conclusion only added to the troubles of the hapless captain who had been stumbling about in the fog. After a Naval Court hearing at the British Consulate in San Francisco, Captain Foster was found guilty of a "grave error in judgment" and lost his master's certificate for one year.

Casey stayed on as lighthouse inspector until 1879, later serving at another lighthouse district. By the time he retired from the navy in 1903, he had risen to the rank of rear admiral. He died in Warm Springs, Virginia, ten years later.

Resurfacing

In 1877, diver James Steele descended on the remains of the *Rydal Hall* and retrieved an anchor and a small amount of chain. In 1971, divers John Koepf and Roy Lee rediscovered the sunken hulk quite by accident while poking around the reef on an abalone hunt. After ninety-five years on the ocean floor, the ill-starred *Rydal Hall* had resurfaced after all.

Initially, it didn't seem that there was much left. "The only thing that remains to shape the boat are a few iron ribs," Lee shrugged. "There are some plates lying around, too, and when we lift off those plates, we sometimes find artifacts underneath." Most of the artifacts were donated to

The "Ships of the World" exhibit, created by the San Mateo County History Museum, includes artifacts from the *Rydal Hall. JoAnn Semones.*

the San Mateo County Historical Society, including a bronze porthole, the bronze scrollwork on the ladder leading to the captain's cabin and a thirty-pound iron ingot.

The duo and their team persevered, working in murky, rough water. Divers raised an enormous anchor, which is still on display in front of a Half Moon Bay seafood restaurant. It required three huge air buoys and a giant crane to lift the fourteen-foot, two-ton anchor out of fifteen feet of water. "The anchor was rusty orange and rubbed clean on its top," newspapers reported, "but on the bottom, it was encrusted with seaweed, barnacles, one star fish and a small abalone."

In 1972, Koepf and Lee located a one-thousand-pound, six-foot deck cannon. Before it was raised successfully, they struggled for two hours, tugging and chaining the heavy cannon to four floating buoys made of old fifty-five-gallon oil drums. Raising the second anchor proved equally challenging.

Surprisingly, the two divers also recovered the ship's bell. For centuries, ships' bells have been used for signaling, keeping time and providing alarm. They're also engraved with the vessel's name, usually with the year the ship was launched. Often, it is the bell that provides the only link to a ship that has slipped into the deep reaches of the sea.

Using a wrecking bar, they labored for four hours before prying the bell away from solidified coal and old ironwork. The duo spent several hours more chipping away at the salt-encrusted, one-hundred-pound bronze bell before uncovering its identifying marks: *Rydal Hall*—1874. "When I spotted a knob sticking up out of the pile, I knew it was something," Koepf exclaimed.

"The bell is priceless. It's not just a hunk of metal or a nice piece of bronze. It's more than that," Koepf noted. "The bell is the essence of a ship. The name and date captures a special moment, the importance of a special time."

TREASURED SHIP'S BELL

In 2014, the "Ships of the World" exhibit was created at the San Mateo County History Museum. On display is the original third-order Fresnel lens from Point Montara Lighthouse, a vibrant oil painting depicting the *Rydal Hall* and a cannon resurrected from the wreck site by John Koepf and Roy Lee.

John Koepf was known far and wide as "Diver John." When he passed away in 2022, he was remembered as "a colorful and memorable personality. He was gregarious, funny, quick with a joke and conversant on a wide range of topics. He will be sorely missed by all who loved him."

The treasured ship's bell still stands watch from the fireplace mantel of John Koepf's home.

CHAPTER 4

AN AWFUL CRASH

ALICE BUCK, SEPTEMBER 26, 1881

An illustrious line of master mariners and adventurous seafaring men stood on the decks of the *Alice Buck*. Once a fading memory, her terrible fate of September 26, 1881, near Point Montara was captured on canvas for all to see.

A SUCCESSFUL SHIP

The *Alice Buck* was meant to sail forever. For good luck, she was named for a granddaughter of Jonathan Buck, who founded Bucksport, one of Maine's earliest ship-building centers. For good measure, her future was put into the hands of several legendary sea captains.

The vessel first entered the water in 1870 at Belfast, Maine, on Penobscot Bay. Built and owned by Captain Henry McGilvery, the *Alice Buck* was 198 feet long and 38 wide and measured 1,425 tons. Coppering of the ship's hull was completed in England, where materials were cheaper.

Although the *Alice Buck* served briefly in the transatlantic cotton trade, the hardy ship spent most of her career shuttling goods to the Far East and to San Francisco. "While she has no fast voyages to her credit," one account declared, "she made good passages and was called a successful ship."

Raised in Stockton, Maine, which lies at the head of Penobscot Bay, Captain McGilvery started sea life as a boy. Rapidly rising through the

Captain Henry McGilvery, a noted shipmaster, built and owned the *Alice Buck*. The vessel first entered the water in 1870. *Penobscot Marine Museum.*

grades from seaman to master, he commanded vessels in the lucrative China trade. He is said to have skippered the first American ship to enter Singapore Harbor. In 1852, at the age of thirty-three, Captain McGilvery retired to embark on shipbuilding ventures in Stockton. Six years later, he moved on to Belfast, where the waterfront was a hub of commercial activity.

Later, he made his home in nearby Hallowell on the banks of the Kennebec River. Captain McGilvery died in 1890 at the age of seventy-one while visiting a daughter in Brooklyn, New York. "He was a man of high character and of remarkable ability," a biographer noted, "both as a shipmaster and a businessman."

MASTER OF FINE SHIPS

Captain McGilvery's choice to command the *Alice Buck* was Captain Phineas Pendleton II of Searsport, Maine. Located just north of Belfast, Searsport was known as "the home of the famous sea captains." During the 1870s and 1880s, the port's seventeen shipyards built two hundred ships and supplied more than 10 percent of the nation's merchant marine deep-water captains.

Captain Pendleton went to sea at age sixteen as a cook and went on to command more than thirty different vessels. Over the years, he became wealthy through successful management of his shipping property and was dubbed a "master and builder of some of the finest ships that sailed the ocean." During the Civil War, he met with large losses at the hands of plundering Confederate privateers. In spite of the setback, he made repeated visits to Washington, D.C., and ultimately received due compensation.

A kindhearted and generous man, Captain Pendleton was renowned for maintaining a productive crew and for taking his vessels safely to port. "A fair illustration to show his kindness," one story goes, "is that he hove his ship to in mid ocean when he was making eight knots an hour at twelve o'clock at night to pick up a monkey that a vicious boy threw overboard."

On land, he was equally regarded for his good nature and was often called "Uncle Phineas." A friend commented, "His hearty and genial manners, storytelling capacity and extended experiences in all parts of the world made him a most entertaining companion."

Captain Pendleton died in 1895 at the age of eighty-nine. "He was a man of striking appearance and many qualities united in making him a profitable friend and acquaintance," an obituary said. "Maine loses one of its old time sea captains of much business capacity and a prominent and highly respected citizen."

INNOVATIVE COMMANDER

After a handful of voyages aboard the *Alice Buck*, Captain Pendleton turned the helm over to his son-in-law. Captain William H. Blanchard had a fine reputation, too, and was innovative when a ship was in trouble.

On a previous vessel, a rudder and steering post was lost in a gale while rounding deadly Cape Horn. "Capt. Blanchard hove to, set his crew to work, rigged a jury rudder and improvised a steering gear," one report asserted. "Then, he sailed around the Horn with this rig, made stops to unload and load cargo at several West Coast ports, and then sailed back to New York on his homemade rudder and steering gear."

He was also a handy man to have around when a doctor was needed. While harbored in Kobe, Japan, during a typhoon, Captain Blanchard noticed distress signals coming from a bark he owned, the *Willard Mudgett*.

Captain Phineas Pendleton II turned command of the *Alice Buck* over to his son-in-law, Captain William H. Blanchard. *Penobscot Marine Museum.*

He learned that Mrs. Dickie, the captain's wife, needed a physician for childbirth, but no one could leave port in such a violent storm.

Captain Blanchard offered his services and shortly presided over the birth of a baby girl. "Capt. Blanchard was experienced," a colleague boasted, "as he had officiated at the birth of five of his children on shipboard." The child became an actress of note, sharing the bill with performers such as James Stewart, Carole Lombard, Cesar Romero and Judy Garland in the 1930s and 1940s. She took the stage named of Clara Blandic—"Clara" for Mrs. Blanchard, "Blan" for Captain Blanchard and "Dic" for her family name.

Unfortunately, Captain Blanchard had his share of misfortunes as well as successes. While on a lengthy voyage from Boston to Valencia, Spain, on the *Bosphorus*, his wife was taken ill and was left in Brazil to return to the United States. Upon arriving in Valencia, Captain Blanchard went ashore to attend to business details. A sudden gale arose, tossing the *Bosphorus* ashore and shattering the ship and her cargo. All but five of the crew drowned, including the first and second mates who were Captain Blanchard's brothers, Edward and Locke.

On another vessel, he survived a fire at sea near Manila, the capital of the Philippines, and soon after retired from sea life. In 1904, Captain Blanchard sailed as a passenger on the *Willard Mudgett*, the same ship on which he had delivered a baby. This time, the vessel was laden with coal and was commanded by his twenty-eight-year-old son, Captain Frederick P. Blanchard. Known as "a good sailer," the ship foundered in a heavy northeast gale while bound from Norfolk, Virginia, to Bangor, Maine. Neither the vessel nor anyone on board was seen or heard from again.

ANCHORS AND APRICOTS

Following Captain Blanchard in 1880 was Captain James R. Herriman. The forty-three-year-old skipper hailed from an old seafaring family in Bangor, Maine, which lies thirty miles up the Penobscot River. He had vast experience commanding barks, brigs and other fill-rigged ships like the *Alice Buck*.

His father, Hezekiah, also a native of Maine, was a respected shipmaster. Upon his father's death, James was taken by his mother to Prospect and then to Winterport, where he attended school. Like other young adventure seekers, he was struck with "sea fever" at the age of fifteen and shipped out as a cabin boy. Herriman became captain of his first vessel at only twenty-two, engaging in merchant trade with the East Indies, Europe and California.

Captain James R. Herriman, another one of the *Alice Buck*'s noted masters, hailed from an old seafaring family. *Penobscot Marine Museum.*

During the Civil War, Captain Herriman commanded a transport ship, conveying troops and heavy munitions for Union naval forces. He carried men, shot and shell to numerous strategic battle locations, including the York River in Virginia and Annapolis Harbor in Maryland. Captain Herriman was also among the Union throng that launched an assault on Fort Jackson and Fort St. Philip for the capture of New Orleans.

The largest city in the Confederacy, New Orleans was threatened by naval forces both to the north and to the south. Trusting that the two forts could thwart any attack from the south, the Confederacy put nearly all its efforts into defending the city to the north.

Meanwhile, the Union mounted a siege on the forts with eighteen thousand soldiers and a fleet of warships, mortar rafts and support vessels. Rebel forces were obliterated, and the subsequent capture of New Orleans was a fatal blow from which the Confederacy never recovered.

After his discharge in 1864, Captain Herriman returned to his old trade in the mercantile business. When he retired from sea life, he was briefly engaged as a marine surveyor in San Francisco. Shortly thereafter, he purchased a ranch near Saratoga in California's fertile Santa Clara Valley, naming it The Anchorage. The bountiful ranch had nearly twenty-three acres of apricots, cherries, peaches and plums. In 1887, the first year of production, competitors observed enviously that "the ranch produced twelve tons of apricots and five tons of peaches, paying eight percent interest on the investment."

BROKEN IN TWO

Filling in for Captain Herriman on the *Alice Buck*'s last passage was Captain Herman Henningsen. Bound for Portland, Oregon, with a cargo destined for the Northern Pacific Railroad, the *Alice Buck* departed New York on April 7, 1881. Building the new railroad, which was completed in 1883, was critical to opening the Pacific Northwest. The 1,780-ton payload, valued at more than $100,000, consisted of 6,668 bars of railroad iron, 1,500 bundles of fishplates for joining or fixing rails, 299 kegs of bolts, 669 railway fasteners called dog spikes and 28 cases of furniture.

On August 28, 1881, the *Alice Buck* collided with a hurricane in the Pacific and sprang a leak in the bow. The following day, a second gale pelted the gurgling ship, pouring more water into the already saturated hold. Desperate, Captain Henningsen steered for San Francisco in hope of repairs. The weary crew worked day and night at the pumps, but the leak only worsened.

At 4:00 p.m. on September 26, the captain calculated the ship to be fifty-five miles southwest of the Golden Gate. On making the coast, not a breath of wind stirred the air. However, a "pretty good sea was running," propelling the *Alice Buck* toward the shores of Half Moon Bay. "Shortly after midnight, under clear and starry skies, the ship struck with an awful crash on the rocks about 1,500 feet from a high bluff," newspapers explained. "She bumped five or six times, bows-on, and at last hit hard and broke in two."

By now, the crew was exhausted, and Captain Henningsen had been on deck steadily for three days and nights. A dingy was launched but upset almost immediately. Two men were washed ashore; one drowned. "That was the last seen of them," a grim-faced captain revealed later.

Another boat containing the two mates, the steward and two seamen was launched but smashed while being lowered. Two of the men scrambled aboard again. The rest disappeared beneath the churning surf. When there was not enough of the crumbling hull to cling to, Captain Henningsen ordered the remaining crew to don life preservers and jump overboard. As one of the deckhouses floated by, the captain and fourteen-year-old cabin boy George Parker seized hold. Young Parker clambered aboard, while the captain floated alongside. Moments later, four others swam over and climbed on as well.

"George asked me if I was afraid and I said no," Captain Henningsen reflected. "He said, 'all right, as long as you keep up and along with me I'll be all right.' As they drifted off I sang out 'good-bye,' and he answered me cheerfully. Before they reached shore the undertow capsized them."

One of the capsized seamen snatched Parker from the surging swells and drifting debris. Unluckily, a heavy wave thrust a chunk of lumber against the lad, knocking him from the sailor's arms. The stout-hearted young cabin boy was swept away by the swirling surf.

The floating wreckage prevented Captain Henningsen from making much headway. After drifting for nine hours in the freezing water, the captain and a handful of others were rescued by the cargo steamer *Salinas*.

The 154-ton vessel—built by James Brennan of Watsonville, California, to haul farm produce, household goods and lime between Santa Cruz and San Francisco—was in the area by sheer chance.

Ashore, two nineteen-year-old farm boys, Silas Hovious and Frank Hale, heroically saved three of the ship's crew. Upon viewing the disastrous scene from the bluff tops, the duo shimmied down an eighty-foot cliff, shouted to those above to throw down a rope and hauled the drowning men from the sea. "We just clumb along somehow. We didn't think much of how we were doing it," the boys mumbled shyly. "We only thought of that sailor in the water."

Sadly, nine of the *Alice Buck*'s twenty crew members drowned. Those lost were First Mate William Barry; Second Mate D. Crocker; cabin boy George Parker; seamen David Black, John Gunnison, Charles Reader and Patrick Welch; the cook; and the steward.

UNIQUE SALVAGE OPERATION

The *Alice Buck* was a total loss. On October 12, the famous Merritt Wrecking Company was dispatched to salvage the iron portion of the cargo. Flying its house flag showing a black stallion in full gallop, the firm was nicknamed the "Black Horse of the Sea." The ironic symbol played on the old term of "white horses," the name given by seafarers to waves breaking into foam.

Captain Israel J. Merritt started the company in 1860, when salvage operations were in their infancy. With $50,000, he established offices on Wall Street in New York, San Francisco and Norfolk, Virginia, under the name of Coast Wrecking Company.

The 1850s and 1860s were a dangerous time for mariners and marine operations around the American continent. Along with the transition from sail to steam came unreliable equipment. The growing needs of commerce, which fueled U.S. expansion, also resulted in larger numbers of vessels plying the sea. Consequently, countless ships foundered, leaving companies like Merritt's to do the harrowing and uncertain work of salvage. "They were a rough-hewn, brash, and stoic group," one writer disclosed, "willing to pit themselves against the sea, their endeavors always high risk, and if fortune smiled, high gain."

Over the years, Coast Wrecking Company saved hundreds of valuable vessels and cargoes, amounting to millions of dollars. The company was known and respected as a pioneer and a leader in the field. "As submarine

The famous Merritt Wrecking Company was sent to salvage cargo from the wrecked *Alice Buck*. *Hudson River Maritime Museum*.

engineers, divers and wreckers, these gentlemen have no equal on this continent," admirers maintained. "They own a fleet of steamers, sailing vessels and pontoons specially built for this work, seaworthy in all weathers, and rigged and fitted regardless of cost."

Initially, Merritt's rugged steamships and crews were able to work in calm waters to raise several hundred tons of cargo. Then the weather changed and a unique plan took shape. In December, a notice appeared in the *Daily Alta* seeking "proposals for the erection of a wharf to the wreck of the ship *Alice Buck*."

In January 1882, the owners of the *Alice Buck* contracted with J.A. Fleming to build a temporary wharf from the shoreline cliffs to the shipwreck site. He worked with Richardson & Thompson Company to construct a wharf that was 1,200 feet long and 54 feet high and "built directly out from the cliff over the rough and rugged boulders." Salvage from the wharf began in July 1882 and continued for more than a year.

One newspaper exclaimed, "This is a piece of engineering skill accomplished and never before attempted on the coast. The great difficulties in the accomplishment of such an undertaking are apparent when it is known that this wharf is built on a solid rock bottom, holes having been drilled in the rock in which to put the piling. Under the efficient superintendency of Mr. Thompson, the task has been well performed."

In December 1884, the wharf was sold to J.A. Fleming, who tore it down and used the timber for other purposes. Exactly how much of the *Alice Buck*'s wreck was salvaged is unknown. What is recorded is the memory of the disaster. It was also captured in the imagination of local artist Galen Wolf.

DOOMED AND DESERTED

Few artists reflect the rampant seas, maritime tragedies and colorful lore of the Pacific coast as uniquely as Galen Wolf. Nowhere are these themes more vividly portrayed than in his noted series, "Legends of the Coastland." Depicted in watercolor mosaic, more than half of the sixteen pieces focus explicitly on maritime subjects. Shipwrecks, whalers, fishermen and even sea monsters appear. Wolf wrote stories to accompany the paintings. These "Legends," especially the shipwreck renderings and tales, offer a rare portal into early California coastal history.

Born in San Francisco in 1889, Galen Russell Wolf grew up with three brothers in Victorian wealth. His father, an enterprising young businessman, built a booming import-export company trading with the Far East. The family home faced the harbor, and sailing ships could be seen easily. On weekends, the family traveled thirty-five miles south by wagon to visit relatives in the seaside village of Half Moon Bay. Wolf stayed happily absorbed in adventurous yarns spun by his grandfather, a veteran seaman who journeyed around Cape Horn in a clipper ship. Wandering the beaches together, they watched eagerly for passing sailing vessels.

Known as the "Dean of San Mateo coastal artists," Wolf was a prolific young watercolorist until 1906, when the San Francisco earthquake and fire destroyed most of his works. Devastated by the loss, he didn't paint again for decades. Wolf turned his interests to the outdoors. Awed by nature's wonders, he fished, hiked through the Sierras and spent twenty years farming and raising a family in the Sacramento Delta.

In 1932, feeling a bit of a castaway, he left his family to return to the simplicity and serenity of Half Moon Bay. "The pulse of life was slow, gentle and rich," Wolf wrote wistfully of his beloved Coastside. "Suddenly, a breath of air comes cool to your face. The scent of the sea is on it—refreshing and exciting."

In about 1950, Wolf began work on "Legends of the Coastland." By that time, cataracts had claimed much of his vision. He created distinctive, highly stylized watercolor mosaic compositions. Wolf's fresh representational art gave the traditional watercolor medium a bold new look. Defined by large-format, free broad brush strokes and strong, rich colors, the "Legends" are dramatic snapshots of coastal life in the 1800s. His paintings, and accompanying narratives, are filled with energy, poignancy and mirth. His innovative approach was nothing short of amazing.

In the "Legends," Wolf brings to life his grandfather's tales of sailing ships and voyages gone awry. With its rocky outcroppings, heavy surf, strong currents and thick fog banks, California's coast was one of the most notoriously dangerous in the world. During the Great Age of Sail, many fine vessels were lost along Pacific shores, including the *Alice Buck*.

Wolf grew up remembering the story of the vessel's unhappy end as his grandfather had told it. He recalled a tale of a disastrous voyage, of a ship overtaken by ferocious waves and of a crew lost in despair. His painting *The Wreck* depicts a young boy's woeful discovery at the water's edge. "It was forlorn," Wolf wrote, "and had the desperate appeal of the doomed and deserted." The once proud ship was now a broken, seaweed-covered hulk. The *Alice Buck* lay forgotten, remembered only by shrieking seabirds.

CHAPTER 5

ONE WRECKING IS ENOUGH

LOS ANGELES, APRIL 21, 1894

The *Los Angeles* saw action during the Civil War, patrolled the desolate territory of Alaska and experienced countless adventures as a passenger and cargo steamer. Her exploits, and the lives of six people, ended when she wrecked at Point Sur on April 21, 1894.

HEAVY HEARTS

Fashioned at Baltimore, Maryland, in 1863 by Fardy & Brothers, the *Los Angeles* was launched under the name *Wayanda*. Although the name was derived from an Indian word meaning the "place of happy hearts," American hearts were heavy. The nation was in the throes of a bloody civil war. Flourishing as the fourth-largest city in the United States when war erupted, Baltimore still held significant strategic value as a shipbuilding and transportation hub.

Providing the nucleus of activity was the shipyard of John T. and Matthew J. Fardy. The brothers were known for their innovative and efficient business methods. Author John G. Gobright observed, "Fardy & Brothers were the first in Baltimore to concentrate the various departments of shipbuilding into one general business, as against previous methods of having work executed at various points. It has been followed by others and given impetus to the business."

Their facilities covered thirty-three thousand square yards with a 250-foot waterfront, sufficient for laying in twenty vessels and building three at a time. They also contained three steam marine railways, including the largest in the city. There, the brothers produced steamships and sailing vessels, both large and small.

The *Wayanda* was one of six Pawtuxet-class tenders ordered for the U.S. Revenue Cutter Service during the Civil War. They were the first steam cutters to enter service since the 1840s. Constructed of oak with iron bracing, the "trim, beautifully modeled" little ships carried six guns, measured 350 tons and were 138 feet long and 27 feet wide. Eventually, their machinery proved to be too cumbersome, thereby shortening each ship's career.

Ordered for the U.S. Revenue Cutter Service during the Civil War, the *Wayanda* carried revenue marines like this dapper young third lieutenant. *U.S. Coast Guard.*

The Revenue Cutter Service, usually assigned to deter smuggling and enforce customs laws as well as to assist mariners in need, was ordered to augment the navy's wartime forces. Created in 1790 as the Revenue-Marine, the service was formed following the American Revolutionary War. With the Treasury Department pressed for money after years of strife, the new organization enforced the collection of import tariff duties as well as other maritime laws. "A few armed vessels judiciously stationed at the entrance of our ports," Secretary of the Treasury Alexander Hamilton asserted, "might at a small expense be made useful sentinels of the laws."

Vessels of the Revenue-Marine persevered through the pirate wars with France from 1798 to 1800, the War of 1812 and the Mexican-American War from 1846 to 1848. By 1832, revenue cutters had also begun conducting winter cruises to assist mariners, including those who were shipwrecked. Renamed in 1862, the Revenue Cutter Service merged with the U.S. Life-Saving Service in 1915 to form the U.S. Coast Guard. The Coast Guard also incorporated the U.S. Lighthouse Service in 1939 and the Navigation and Steamboat Inspection Service in 1942.

COTTON AND SEALS

Finished at a cost of $103,000, the *Wayanda* carried a complement of forty-one officers and crew. She completed several general assignments under the command of Captain J.A. White. In February 1865, she was ordered to Savannah, Georgia, to protect a convoy of the "Cotton Fleet." The flotilla comprised Union ships carrying thousands of cotton bales confiscated from Southern plantations. Cotton was a valuable commodity, prized by the burgeoning textile industry in England and in Northern American states.

Shortly after the end of the war, she was placed at the disposal of Chief Justice Salmon P. Chase for a fact-finding mission to Southern states. Participating was journalist Whitelaw Reid, later a politician and longtime editor of the *New York Tribune*. In a memoir of the trip, Reid described their departure. "We had started in the night, were well out on the ocean, a pretty heavy sea was running, and the nettlesome little *Wayanda* was giving us a taste of her qualities," he wrote. "Nothing could exceed the beauty of her plunges fore and aft, and lurches from port to starboard, but the party was sadly lacking in enthusiasm."

The *Wayanda* was ordered to the port of San Francisco in June 1866 and then on to Alaskan waters in 1868. Secretary of State William Seward had initiated the purchase of Alaska from Russia the previous year, convincing President Andrew Johnson and the U.S. Senate to buy 600,000 square miles of howling wilderness for $7.2 million. Referring to the deal as "Seward's Folly" and "Andrew Johnson's Polar Bear Garden," most viewed the region as "a barren waste." To everyone's surprise, the investment paid off when gold was discovered. Waves of settlers and fortune hunters flocked to Alaska, some intent on breaking the law.

Alaska sprouted as a land of both bounty and danger. For many years, members of the Revenue Cutter Service shouldered responsibilities far beyond that of enforcing revenue laws. They were a marine police force, charged with administering the new, untamed territory. They helped build and maintain Alaska's teeming towns too. In annual cruises from the lower forty-eight states, cutters like the *Wayanda* brought everything from the mails to medical assistance to lumber for courthouses and churches.

The cutters also patrolled Alaska's fisheries and whaling grounds and controlled sealing on the neighboring Pribilov Islands. Sealing was legal, relatively easy and immensely profitable. A single voyage with a load of seal furs could net $10,000, considerably more than an average worker's yearly income. Usually, the hunt was a matter of driving the animals to a

After the Civil War, the *Wayanda* was sent to Alaska to oversee the untamed territory and control fishing, whaling and sealing activities. *U.S. Navy*.

killing ground on the islands during the summer season. Poachers sought to maximize their profits by pelagic sealing, or killing the pinnipeds at sea, along their migratory route between Alaska and San Diego.

The result proved disastrous. In 1867, the northern fur seal population was more than 4 million. In 1868, raids killed half a million of the mammals. The Treasury Department sent revenue cutters and agents to halt the slaughter. In subsequent years, regulations were enacted to control sealing on the islands and on the migratory routes. The Revenue Cutter Service became the key enforcer of these laws, and consequently, prevented the species' extinction.

Sometime in the late 1860s, the *Wayanda* was subject to a "major rebuilding" with some thirty feet being added to her hull length. She was decommissioned in October 1873, sold to Goodall, Nelson & Perkins Steamship Company and renamed the *Los Angeles*.

"The government sold her because of her machinery, not on account of the hull, which is sound," Charles Goodall said of the purchase. "She had an old-fashioned propeller, and her machinery weighed many times what it should. The new modern machinery, which we put in, developed the same power at a great saving in fuel."

EVENTFUL ODYSSEYS

Now a passenger and cargo steamer, the *Los Angeles* made countless trips along the California coast. Usually, the voyages were routine. On any given journey, she transported dozens of passengers, hundreds of barrels of lime, thousands of shakes and other building materials and even an occasional horse. Other odysseys proved more eventful.

With Captain Sholl at the helm in February 1878, the *Los Angeles* broke a shaft at Tillamook, Oregon, and was given up for lost. Somehow, First Mate Jeff Howell landed on the beach and made his way fifty miles overland to Astoria, where he secured a tug that towed the vessel into port.

While on her regular route in 1883, the *Los Angeles* rushed to the rescue of a fog signal keeper, his assistant and two friends. According to the *San Mateo County Gazette*, "One of the most appalling accidents that ever occurred on this coast happened at Año Nuevo Island."

Located fifty-five miles south of San Francisco, Año Nuevo is both an island and a point. In the 1800s, the island was accessible only at low tide. At other times, it was reached from the point in a dinghy. In 1872, a fog signal station with a steam whistle was placed on Año Nuevo Island. A keepers' dwelling was constructed at the southern end of the island, with a wooden walkway running north to the fog signal station. A lighthouse was erected in 1890.

Two local farmers, Clayton and Frank Pratt, were in the habit of taking a small boat and visiting the keepers on Año Nuevo Island most Sundays. Although the crossing was rough on April 14, they reached their destination without incident. Having spent the day pleasantly, the brothers began the return trip to the mainland accompanied by keeper Henry Colburn and assistant keeper Bernard Ashley. Rather than taking the usual course by the "beacon stake," they started on what was known as the "straight cut," a distance of about half a mile.

In the middle of the journey, breakers swamped their vessel. The men tried desperately to bail water from the beleaguered little boat, but they drifted out to sea. Another unruly wave rolled over them, taking them from sight. Witnessing the events, Mrs. Colburn and Mrs. Ashley hurried to the boathouse, attempted to launch the remaining lifeboat, but found it too heavy to move. Hoping to attract the attention of a passing vessel, the two women hoisted a distress flag and sounded the fog signal.

Luckily, the *Los Angeles* heard the fog signal, lowered a boat to the island and embarked on a search of the area. When nothing was found, the *Los Angeles* steamed six miles down the coast in the hopes of recovering the lost men. Lighthouse inspector George W. Coffin stated later, "The coast was searched up and down and finding no trace of the boat or bodies, the matter was reported to me."

In 1891, two "Salvation Army lassies" were among the passengers aboard the *Los Angeles*. To bid them a bon voyage, a number of male and female Salvation Army soldiers gathered on the San Francisco wharf and began

Decommissioned in 1873, the *Wayanda* was sold, rebuilt as a passenger and cargo steamer and renamed the *Los Angeles*. *San Francisco Maritime National Historical Park.*

singing hymns and chanting war cries. The resulting din drowned out the voice of the ship's skipper, Captain Hannah.

"The sailors, not being able to hear anything, above their shouting of hallelujahs, failed to comprehend an order to let go one of the lines," the *San Francisco Chronicle* commented. "The steamer, caught by the tide, swung on top of a scow, doing, however, but little damage. Capt. Hannah treated the Army to a dose of opinion freely expressed in nautical language."

DAMPENED SPIRITS

On April 20, 1894, no one knew that the *Los Angeles'* escapades were about to come to an end. En route from Newport Beach, the steamer was bound for San Francisco's gala Midwinter International Exposition. The event was the first American-sponsored world exposition held west of the Mississippi River. Aboard were thirty-six crew and forty-nine passengers, most in a festive mood. Unfortunately, the voyage would more than dampen their spirits.

The ship made a routine call at San Simeon to add eighty tons of wool to the existing cargo of beans, butter, cheese, grain and oranges. San Simeon Bay had become a substantial port by the early 1870s, exporting lumber, farm produce, wool and cinnabar, an ore mined for its mercury. Upon departure, Captain Herman D. Leland remained at the bridge until passing the distinctive white rock of Piedras Blancas Lighthouse, erected just north of San Simeon in 1875.

Having been on deck for twelve hours, Captain Leland retired for a nap and set a "compass course," which was meant to keep the *Los Angeles* out of danger until passing treacherous Point Sur. Before entering his cabin, the captain left orders with Third Officer Roger Ryfkogel to rouse him when they reached Cooper's Point, about five miles southeast of Point Sur.

"The weather was the best we have had for some time," a member of the crew noted. "Generally, we encounter strong winds after leaving San Simeon, but this trip was an exception to the rule, and we all counted on getting ahead of time."

As the *Los Angeles* cruised up the coast, Ryfkogel failed to recognize Cooper's Point. Why he didn't see Point Sur's light is unknown. Having passed the promontory, he altered the ship's course, hoping to gain calmer water. Instead, the vessel struck a submerged pinnacle of rocks seven hundred yards west of Point Sur. A passenger, Captain T.J. MacGenn of the wrecker *Whitelaw*, "was greatly surprised to find that the lighthouse was on their left and not the right."

"The first shock was not severe, and I did not think anything serious had happened until the second shock wave," recalled E.S. Tunison, a traveler aboard the *Los Angeles*. "Almost instantly, the order came for the passengers to go on deck. One woman with a child in her arms rushed into my stateroom and fell in a faint."

Dressed only in their night clothes, the passengers clambered to the upper deck. As the crew distributed blankets and life preservers, Captain Leland shouted orders to lower the lifeboats. "You could hardly hear yourself think for the shrieks of the women and children," a seaman acknowledged. "It was almost impossible for the orders of the captain to be heard in the confusion. It seemed as though every officer on board had a different order to give."

Despite the chaos, most of the passengers were loaded into the lifeboats quickly. A few of the boats were dispatched to hail the steamer *Eureka* on her way south. After flailing around in a half-swamped dinghy, one soggy troupe spotted the lights of the steamship and were pulled aboard. One of the passengers, J.H. Cummings, wore his battered, water-soaked hat as if it were a crown. "This is the hat that bailed water from our boat," he chortled. "Without it, we might have sunk."

Other lifeboats headed directly for shore. In one, water began seeping through a hole near the keel. Although lifeboats have a hole in the bottom to drain any accumulated rain water when they are stowed on deck, they also have a plug that is used when the boat is needed in an emergency. In this case, the plug was missing. When the crew considered deserting the craft, Mrs. Frank Ey, a passenger, thought otherwise. "She placed her hand over the aperture while others bailed out the boat," a local newspaper explained, "and a sailor whittled a plug to stop the leakage."

WORSE POSSIBLE PLACE

Still left on the deck of the lacerated *Los Angeles* were Captain Leland, Second Officer Ward, the first assistant engineer, fireman Tom Nolan and a handful of passengers. As the vessel plunged into the sea, Ward called out, "All hands to the rigging—every man for himself."

The ship lurched onto her side but settled for a time. Above the roiling surf, only the top portion of her masts remained visible. The men scrambled high into the rigging but were soon exhausted. "It was at this time that three of the more unfortunate were thrown into the sea," one seaman declared. "The sight of the men drowning before my eyes was simply horrible."

When all seemed hopeless, a lifeboat appeared out of the darkness. Led by Captain MacGenn, the boat carried the remaining survivors ashore. Sadly, one of those in this waterlogged little band died in the lifeboat before reaching land. Another expired a few moments later on the wreck-strewn beach. "The poor boy, we could do nothing for him," a sailor lamented. "He was too far gone and died in my arms."

The disaster occurred in full view of Point Sur's keepers J.F. Ingersoll and Peter C. Nelson, who rushed to the rescue. The keepers and their wives, including Mrs. Ida Pate Nelson, turned the keepers' residence into a makeshift hospital, furnishing the survivors with "well-cooked food, dry clothing and stimulants." One survivor asserted, "I was treated handsomely by the folks there, but I must say that God Almighty never made a worse possible place for a wreck than this Point Sur."

Dr. John Roberts was summoned as well. The doctor ministered to people up and down the isolated coast and had also brought Keeper Nelson's son, Ernest, and daughter, Myrtle, into the world. Dr. Roberts and his horse, Daisy, made the thirty-mile trip from Monterey to Point Sur in three and a half hours, the fastest time anyone had ever made the trek over the rugged wagon road. When he arrived, Dr. Roberts found "150 people thrashing around in the surf, some trying to climb rocks, some already dying." He spent three days and three nights, without rest or sleep, treating the injured and tending to the dead.

He later submitted a bill for $150 to the steamship company for services rendered. It was rejected as too high, so Dr. Roberts raised his bill to $300. When the firm continued to refuse payment, he threatened to impound one of the company's ships docked in Monterey. According to one source, "This brought prompt payment and much delight to the good doctor."

NEGLIGENCE AND CARELESSNESS

The Monterey Coroner's Office lost no time in conducting an investigation into the cause of the wreck. Not surprisingly, opinions varied. Captain Leland testified that the light at Point Sur could be plainly seen that evening. "Had my orders been obeyed, no accident would have occurred," he growled. "They were disregarded, and here we are."

Third Office Ryfkogel attributed the accident to a strong current that sent the vessel toward shore. "I obeyed my orders to the best of my ability.

A contentious investigation followed the *Los Angeles*'s mishap. Captain Herman Leland (front) and Third Officer Roger Ryfkogel (right) were held responsible. *From the* San Francisco Morning Call.

I was not changing course. I was simply trying to make the course given me," he claimed. "I was just about to go and call the captain when the ship struck the rocks, and I thought we had not yet made Cooper's Point."

First Officer Charles Gray, called a hero for saving nine men who had jumped overboard, provided the most damaging observations. "The wreck can be attributed only to criminal negligence, or gross ignorance, on the part of the officer in command at the time," he insisted. No officer can change the course of a ship without consulting with the captain."

The coroner's jury concluded that Ryfkogel was guilty of criminal negligence and carelessness, and he was taken into custody. The *Santa Cruz Sentinel* commented, "Third Mate Roger Ryfkogel of the *Los Angeles* lies in the strong jail of Monterey under detention pending a charge of manslaughter."

Charges were dropped later on the grounds of insufficient evidence. However, a subsequent investigation by U.S. inspectors E.T. Talbot and W.A. Phillips revoked the licenses of both Ryfkogel and Captain Leland. Ryfkogel was found guilty of disobeying a standing order and the captain of setting the wrong course.

A final tally showed that six people perished in the tragedy. They included one crew member and five passengers, including a young boy. Others were scarred for life. "Somehow, I feel as if I don't care to go to sea again," a sailor shrugged. "One wrecking is enough for me."

CHAPTER 6

A JINX SHIP

NEW YORK, MARCH 13, 1898

The *T.F. Oakes* was one of the most notorious ships to ever sail. Her reputation failed to improve even after she was renamed the *New York*. The beleaguered ship came to a bitter end, wrecking at Half Moon Bay on March 13, 1898.

NOTHING IS RIGHT

Only three large full-rigged iron ships were built in the United States: the *Tillie E. Starbuck*, the *T.F. Oakes* and the *Clarence S. Bement*. Unfortunately, the career of each of these vessels was so discouraging that it marked the end of American efforts to construct iron sailing vessels almost before it began. The *T.F. Oakes* received the greatest notoriety, for her odyssey was anything but tranquil.

Named after Thomas Fletcher Oakes, president of Northern Pacific Railway, the *T.F. Oakes* was constructed in 1883 for William H. Starbuck, a prominent New York shipping merchant. Starbuck was impressed by the theoretical superiority of iron over wood as a shipbuilding material and dreamed of revolutionizing American shipping. Using iron, he explained to the local press, had "the benefit of increased carrying capacity, better insurance, and stronger ships."

Built by the newly formed American Shipbuilding Company of Philadelphia, the *T.F. Oakes* was 255 feet long and nearly 41 feet wide and

One of three full-rigged iron sailing ships built in America, the *T.F. Oakes* became one of the most notorious vessels to ever sail. *Mariners' Museum.*

measured 1,997 tons. Valued at $135,000, the vessel was painted black and white and had a round stern, two decks, three masts and an eagle on the bow. Veteran seaman Peter Johnson called her "the finest looking sailing ship I had ever seen."

The *T.F. Oakes* was delivered rapidly, entering the water just 150 days after the keel was laid. At her launching, Henry H. Gorringe, a former naval commander and head of American Shipbuilding, boasted, "I have leased this shipyard for the purpose of building the merchant marine of the future. Our successful launch today is only a beginning. No yard in this country has finer facilities for doing work expeditiously and well than we do here."

Sadly, the iron ship would never live up to everyone's high praise. She proved a heavy, dull and slow sailer, as well as an unlucky vessel. She was top heavy, carrying eleven thousand square yards of canvas, and when she passed under New York's Brooklyn Bridge, all three of her masts had to be lowered.

With Captain John B. Clift at the helm, her first voyage broke all records for the longest passage, a leisurely 195 days, from New York to San Francisco. Bound for China on her second voyage, the *T.F. Oakes* was caught in a typhoon, thrown on her beam ends and nearly wrecked. A passing steamer rescued the crippled ship and towed her into Hong Kong.

"The trouble started in the model before the keel was laid; it continued in the building, in the placing of the masts and the proportioning of spars and cutting of canvas," one observer declared. "Nothing is right and in balance, and no matter how you drive or jockey in handling a ship, you can never get out of her what is not in her."

SHIPBOARD INJUSTICES

For the next decade, the *T.F. Oakes* plodded the seas, earning the reputation of a ship on which "blows were plenty and food was scarce." When a new skipper, Captain Edward W. Reed, took command, her record failed to improve. Captain Reed had a stormy career aboard the vessel and was often accused of abusing his crew. Broadly publicized in the "Red Record" of the *Coast Seamen's Journal*, the charges did little to enhance the ship's esteem.

The *Coast Seamen's Journal* was first published in 1887 by the Coast Seaman's Union, then two years old and with an active membership of two thousand men. The *Journal* had always run stories of shipboard injustices, but a new feature appeared in 1894. A litany of brutality cases was grouped together in a column called the "Red Record." The article was subtitled "Being a Bare Outline of Some of the Cases of Cruelty Perpetrated Upon American Seamen." It bore as its trademark a red ink engraving of a fist with a bloody belaying pin.

"Something must be done to wipe out this shameful blot upon an honorable profession," Walter J. Macarthur, the *Journal*'s editor, stressed. "In the name of justice and humanity we call upon our readers to do what lies in their power, particularly by making the facts widely known, toward the abolition of the seagoing Legrees!"

After a voyage in 1893, Captain Reed was charged with cruelty. Six seamen gave evidence in court and displayed wounds they claimed he inflicted. Although many spectators in the court expressed indignation and confidence of a conviction, Captain Reed made no defense. The jury returned the verdict that "a shipmaster has the right to beat a seaman who is unruly." The *Coast Seamen's Journal* commented that the case demonstrated "the dangerous powers vested in ships' officers."

Following another crossing in 1895, Captain Reed was charged with "extreme brutality and murder." The crew testified that Frederick Owens, an able seaman who complained of sickness, was assaulted, dragged out of the forecastle and compelled to work during bitterly cold weather off Cape

Horn. They contended that Captain Reed ordered Owens to "walk the deck, even though he couldn't work." Owens was given no medical attention except a dose of salts and a mustard plaster and died two days later.

However, the captain had his own version of events. He countered that Owens "was a lazy fellow" who had attempted to strike Captain Reed. In self-defense, he shoved the man onto a pile of sails. In the end, the court found insufficient evidence against the shipmaster, and Captain Reed was acquitted.

ALL HOPE ABANDONED

A particularly disastrous passage from Hong Kong to New York occurred in 1896. On July 5, the *T.F. Oakes* cleared Hong Kong with a cargo of hides and skins and a contingent of twenty-seven, including Captain Reed and his wife, Hannah. Born in the coal region of Pottsville, Pennsylvania, in 1837, Captain Reed shipped out as a sailor at age seventeen. Prior to taking over command of the sailing ship *T.F. Oakes* in 1888, he served as master of the *T.F. Oakes'* "sister-ship," *Tillie E. Starbuck*, for four years.

Hannah Reed was no stranger to the sea or to the hardships of shipboard life. Born in New Hampshire in 1847, she sailed with her husband on numerous voyages on both of the iron ships. During that time, she learned everything about handling a ship. She also understood the changing temperaments of the sea and the risks of long, arduous journeys. On this voyage, she was described in newspapers as "a fine, strong woman of fifty. Her face is thin, worn by what she has been through. Yet, her clear, gray eyes and the firm set of her jaw prove her determination."

A week out of Hong Kong, the ship *T.F. Oakes* was caught in a succession of typhoons that blew her five hundred miles off course to the northeast. Captain Reed changed the usual course around the Cape of Good Hope in South Africa and continued the journey sailing toward Cape Horn in South America. The new route was five to seven thousand miles farther.

"After many never-ending days and nights we found ourselves battling gales. Head gales mostly, with bitter weather, driving rain, icy sleet and blinding snow. Always soaked to the skin and always hungry. God in Heaven, how hungry we were," seaman Hans Arro recalled. "With huge waves continually flooding over her decks, the ship was wet and cold. And how cold and dank was our leaky foc'sle with no stove to warm and dry it."

The voyage took more than eight months. During that time, Captain Reed was partially paralyzed by a stroke, and many of the weary crew fell

Hannah Reed took over the helm of the *T.F. Oakes* during a disastrous passage from Hong Kong to New York in 1896. *From the* New York Journal.

ill with scurvy. The disease progressed rapidly, killing six men and disabling everyone else but the second mate and Mrs. Reed. The tormented ship crawled up the Brazilian coast with Mrs. Reed at the helm. Daily rations were cut to six ounces of bread and a gulp of water per person. While off Trinidad, another vessel, the *Governor Robie*, supplied a few provisions, but conditions continued to worsen.

"The man Abrams could hardly speak and his legs were so swollen that it was a wonder that he could drag himself about the deck. The Captain and Third Officer Eagan were too helpless to leave their bunks and Mrs. Reed was almost as bad," one account revealed. "Forward, eleven men lay starving and helpless in their bunks, most of them toothless owing to the scurvy. They were so weak that they slid from side to side on their straw mattresses on every roll of the ship."

On March 15, 1897, the blue glare of the stricken vessel's distress signal was sighted by the British tanker *Kasbek*. In reply to a hail from the *Kasbek*, a voice from the *T.F. Oakes* shouted back, "Can't heave to—all dead and sick. For heaven's sake stand by and send us a boat."

A handful of the *Kasbek*'s crew remained aboard the *T.F. Oakes*. For three days, the iron ship staggered alongside the tanker. When the heavy winds and seas subsided, the *Kasbek* attached a towing hawser to pull the *T.F. Oakes* into port. Finally, on March 21, anchor was dropped near a New York quarantine station. By this time, the *T.F. Oakes* was 249 days out from China and listed as missing. According to one account, "All hope for her reappearance had been abandoned."

Captain Reed was charged with maliciously withholding food from the crew. During a trial before a New York District Court, members of Captain Reed's crew gave vivid accounts of deprivation and beatings and read letters written by sailors who had died during the voyage. Many were unable to walk unassisted to the witness stand. Captain Reed himself limped into the courtroom. Paralysis still affected his speech, but he denied all allegations.

Hannah Reed stated that the men were "impossible to please." She said they grumbled about everything, were unruly and often "flailed their fists" at the captain. The case was dismissed on the grounds that due to the extreme length of the passage, shortage of food was unavoidable. However, that did not end the dispute. Eight sailors pressed charges against Captain Reed for neglect to supply proper and sufficient food. They were each awarded $362.25.

For taking the helm and staying the course on such an onerous journey, newspapers hailed Hannah as a true heroine. For her skill in steering the vexed ship, Lloyd's of London, the largest maritime underwriter in the world, awarded Hannah its Silver Medal for Meritorious Service. One story emphasized, "She stood at the wheel as sailors died. Had she not been brave, steadfast and helpful, this story might never have been told. The *T.F. Oakes* might be resting on the bottom of the sea or drifting a derelict, a floating coffin, over the Atlantic Ocean."

After forty-four years, Captain Reed retired from sea life. The following winter, the Reed home in Haverhill, Massachusetts, burned to the ground. The Reeds escaped in their night clothes, but the captain caught pneumonia and died in March 1899. The cause of the fire was never known, but it was rumored that some of his crew had a hand in it as retaliation for his treatment of them. Perhaps after the final trauma of losing her home and her husband, Hannah Reed preferred a reclusive life. Nothing more is documented about her endeavors.

A MISERABLE TIME

While the *T.F. Oakes* was at sea, she was purchased by Lewis Luckenbach. His steamship company was one of the most long-lived and successful shipping enterprises in the United States. After building his fortune by pioneering tug-and-barge transport of coal from Norfolk, Virginia, to New England, Luckenbach became a major force in the intercoastal trade between the Atlantic and Pacific shores.

Luckenbach received delivery of the *T.F. Oakes* once she reached port. He was no doubt stunned by the unexpected lengthy voyage and the subsequent courtroom debacle. Realizing that it would be impossible to lure sailors to a vessel with a checkered history, Luckenbach changed the ship's name to the *New York*. He also hired the experienced shipmaster Thomas Peabody, who "was regarded as a high class navigator, a driver and a strict disciplinarian."

After a complete overhaul, the ship sailed from New York on May 18, 1897, bound for Shanghai and then Hong Kong. The trip went without incident. On the return voyage to San Francisco, the vessel carried Captain Peabody; his wife, Clara; their eight-year-old daughter, Claire; twenty crew;

The *T.F. Oakes* was renamed the *New York*. Captain Thomas Peabody sailed with his wife, Clara, and daughter, Claire. *San Mateo County History Museum*.

and a rich cargo of coffee, dry goods, firecrackers, flour, garlic, green beans, hemp, peanut oil, pineapples, porcelains, rattan furniture, silk, spices, tapioca rice, tea, tobacco and wine.

Unhappily, the vessel's newfound good luck was fleeting. Leaving Hong Kong Harbor on January 14, 1898, the *New York* was plagued by unceasing storms. "From the first day we had a miserable time. Our ship ran into storm after storm," Claire Peabody wrote later. "The crew, disheartened, whispered among themselves that maybe the *New York* was a jinx-ship. Some of the men even went so far as to predict they would never see San Francisco harbor again."

About nine hundred miles off the California coast, the vessel ran into a furious squall that snapped the main mast. With no extra spars aboard, the crew did their best to patch the damage, but it was not enough. "Her steering had been bad enough before," seaman Paul Scharrenberg stated, "but from that night the good ship could not be made to readily respond to her helm."

Gales continued to batter the struggling ship. In the early morning hours of March 13, 1898, the *New York* became lost in heavy fog and was driven broadside onto the beach at Half Moon Bay. The misguided vessel missed her destination by a mere thirty miles. "The only explanation I can give of the disaster is the fact of the extremely contrary current along the coast at that time," Captain Peabody shrugged. "The seaman aloft could see nothing. I thought I was a little farther north, and that Point Bonita Light, for which I was looking, was on my bow."

Over the next few hours, the *New York* settled in the sand about two hundred yards from shore. Captain Peabody and his crew made preparations to launch the two undamaged lifeboats. Carrying the captain's wife and daughter and eight men, the first boat narrowly escaped destruction against the *New York*'s iron hull when it filled with water from the crashing waves and nearly capsized. Scores of local residents who had dashed to the scene formed a human chain into the sea and snatched the helpless group from the undercurrent.

A second boat with ten crew was successfully launched, but not without mishap. Heavy seas hurled the ship's cook between the craft and the davits, fracturing his leg at the knee. Three men, including Captain Peabody, still remained aboard the *New York*. Several attempts were made to launch a boat back to rescue them, but the turbulent surf prevailed. Only at daybreak did the captain and the last of his crew manage to reach shore.

The tug *Reliance*, under the command of Captain Gilbert Brokaw, was dispatched from San Francisco, but heavy surf and strong southwest winds made it impossible to get closer than half a mile from the stranded ship. "The beach at Half Moon Bay," observed W.C. Callip, the *New York*'s first mate, "will in all probability, be her graveyard."

However, the sturdy tug averted another disaster. Bound from San Francisco to Cork, Ireland, with a cargo of wheat, the British four-master *Clan Galbraith* came dangerously close to where the *New York* lay. Captain Brokaw hailed the vessel and kept the *Reliance* by its side until it passed safely. "It was touch and go with her," he acknowledged. "I delayed my departure for San Francisco, thinking every minute she would require my assistance."

A SHAMEFUL EPITAPH

Meanwhile, the ill-fated *New York* sank deeper and deeper until she lay buried in twenty-three feet of sand. By March 16, the iron ship was filled water, the main hatch was broken, cabin windows were smashed, furniture was awash, the forecastle was completely gutted and the vessel had a decided list. "The tapioca rice in her hold had burst the deck and might force the hull apart," the *New York Maritime Register* reported. "The vessel had fallen over to starboard and the seas were breaking over her. Her back was broken."

The *New York*'s cargo, worth $500,000, was sold at auction for $5,600 on March 24. Two days later, U.S. Customs officials set up a crude shanty on the beach. The structure was composed primarily of the ship's hatches that had washed ashore. Tents were also erected and three cables were rigged between the ship and the shore. "The inspectors at the scene found it necessary to keep a close watch upon the goods saved from the wreck," one newspaper disclosed. "The beach is infested with thieves, who prowl in the night as well as during the day."

Before the customs inspectors arrived to take possession of the cargo, local residents claimed many souvenirs from the ship. "My father, along with other young men, went out to claim relics," Mrs. Ethel Knapp Neate confessed. "I have in my home the big arm chair taken from the captain's cabin."

Several boxes of hand-painted chinaware also disappeared, finding their way into Half Moon Bay homes. Some still survive in excellent condition today. Horace Nelson took possession of the ship's bell. After tolling out so many hours at sea, it hung on the water tower of his ranch, where it was used to call the hands to their meals.

Along with six of his crew, Captain Peabody made several trips to the doomed vessel to bring ashore personal effects of the sailors and his daughter's

During a voyage in 1898, the *New York* wrecked at Half Moon Bay and sank into the sand. *San Mateo County History Museum.*

pet birds. Peabody and his family took such a liking to the Coastside that they settled in nearby Moss Beach for several years.

The following month, the *New York* was stripped of all her fittings and ornamentation. Everything of value was taken, leaving her a skeleton in the sand. Soon, all traces of the infamous ship vanished. Seaman Paul Scharrenberg, who served on the *New York* and later became editor of the *Coast Seamen's Journal*, declared, "The wreckers and breakers made scrap iron out of her and left her a more or less unpleasant memory to deepwater sailors the world over."

It was a shameful epitaph for a scandalous ship.

CHAPTER 7

BEFUDDLED BY THE COASTLINE

CITY OF FLORENCE, MARCH 19, 1900

Sometimes even the best-built ship grows tired and troubled. The venerable *City of Florence* wrecked on March 19, 1900, just two hundred yards north of where the infamous *New York* met her demise.

GREAT SHIPBUILDING CITY

Originally a small salmon fishing village at a crossing point on the sparkling River Clyde, Glasgow, Scotland, grew into one of the greatest shipbuilding cities on earth. From the early 1800s into the 1900s, the banks of the Clyde sprouted with shipyards where tens of thousands of men built magnificent ships.

Stretching more than one hundred miles, the Clyde was naturally a shallow waterway, often only two feet at low tide. In 1768, a sequence of dykes was built, narrowing the channel and greatly increasing the flow of water, which in turn scoured the bed and deepened the river. In 1812, the Clyde's entry into the world of shipbuilding began when the twenty-eight-ton paddle steamer *Comet*, Europe's first seagoing steam ship, was launched at Port Glasgow.

An ad in local newspapers invited passengers to board the new vessel: "The subscriber, having at much expense, fitted up a handsome vessel to ply upon the River Clyde from Glasgow, to sail by the power of air, wind and steam, intends that the vessel shall leave Broomielaw on Tuesdays, Thursdays

The *City of Florence* was designed at the eminent shipbuilding center on the River Clyde in Glasgow, Scotland. *State Library of South Australia.*

and Saturdays about mid-day, or such hour thereafter as may answer from the state of the tide, and to leave Greenock on Mondays, Wednesdays and Fridays in the morning to suit the tide." The fare was "four shillings for the best cabin and three shillings for the second."

The *Comet* made a delivery voyage from Port Glasgow twenty-one miles upriver to Broomielaw and then sailed the twenty-four miles down to Greenock, making five miles per hour against a headwind. The success of this service quickly inspired competition.

Due to its location on the western part of the country, Glasgow was well positioned to send cargo to the West Indies and to the United States. Accordingly, shipyards were established on the Clyde at an extraordinary rate. Soon the river gained a reputation for producing the best vessels in Britain and emerged as the world's preeminent shipbuilding center. "Clydebuilt" became a byword for excellence, durability and reliability.

SUPERIOR SHIPS

One of the premier shipbuilders of the day was Charles Connell. After serving an apprenticeship with Robert Steele & Company, he managed the shipyard of Alexander Stephen & Sons. Both were well-established and respected firms on the Clyde. In 1861, Connell formed his own firm, initially concentrating on sailing ships.

The enterprise, known as C. Connell & Company, was successful beyond his wildest dreams, delivering vessels like the *City of Florence*, as well as passenger and cargo ships, to customers around the world. His famous sailing ships include the *Balclutha*, now on display at the San Francisco Maritime Museum. "Well known for high quality," his passenger and cargo vessels sailed in the fleets of countless international lines.

The shipyard passed from the Connell family's ownership in 1968 to become part of the Upper Clyde Shipbuilders, finally closing in 1980 after 119 years of shipbuilding. More than five hundred ships had been launched under the Connell name.

Although the *City of Florence* was built by Charles Connell, she was owned by George Smith, another Scotsman. In partnership with his brother, Robert, Smith established the City Line of Calcutta in 1840 to support their cotton manufacturing firm's expanding trade with India.

George Smith owned the *City of Florence*. He established a popular fleet of ships known as the City Line. *James MacLehose*.

After purchasing several ready-made ships, they resolved that any further additions to their fleet should be vessels built to their own specifications. "This resolution was steadily adhered to, with the result that a superior type of ship was built," reports said, "and the vessels of the firm speedily acquired fame for their speed, safety and regularity."

In 1847, construction of their first vessel was contracted with Tod & Macgregor of Glasgow. When she was launched the following year, the brothers wished to acknowledge the port and dubbed her the *City of Glasgow*. The succeeding ships of their fleet were named after other cities and came to be known as the City Line.

Within a decade, the line was making voyages to Chile and the West Indies, Australia and New Zealand. In 1871, the company added steamers to its burgeoning fleet. "For economy of working, carrying power, and speed suited to the trade in which they are employed, the steamers are regarded as holding a foremost place amongst steamship lines," an admirer bragged. "Their safety is proverbial and the well-known preference they command in both goods and passengers is deserved."

George Smith died in 1876, three years after his brother passed away, leaving the business to his son, George Jr. A biographer noted, "He was remembered as a man who was "of sharp, quick, and powerful intellect with immense capacity for work.""

UNLUCKY VOYAGE

The *City of Florence*, a three-masted sailing ship, slid down the ways of the River Clyde in 1867. She had a length of 227 feet, a beam of 34 feet and a depth of 22 feet and measured 1,246 tons. Although she had several masters, Captain William "Jock" Leask, who commanded her from 1884 to 1899, was at the helm for almost half her life.

Born in the Orkney Islands off the northern tip of Scotland in 1851, William Leask served the usual apprenticeship before going to sea and taking command of his first ship. He was described by one biographer as "a man of medium height though broad to the point of ungainliness, it needed only a glance at the keen gray eyes peering from beneath bushy eyebrows, the determined set of a square lower jaw, to note a man accustomed to command. A quick, alert turn of the head, the lift of shoulders as he walked, arms swinging in seamanlike balance, and the trick of pausing to glance at the weather sky, marked the sailing shipmaster, the man to whom thought and action must be one."

An experienced skipper, Captain Leask rounded treacherous Cape Horn forty-two times. One of his worst trips aboard the *City of Florence* occurred on a voyage from Antwerp, Belgium, carrying 9,590 barrels of cement consigned to Mever, Wilson, & Company. The vessel encountered twenty-eight days of successive gales and hurricanes. Captain Leask stated simply, "It was an unlucky voyage throughout."

The ship's main mast splintered. Sail after sail flew away in shreds. Mountainous waves pounded the beleaguered vessel, smashing the lifeboats and damaging cabin doors. Deck fastenings were ripped from their ring bolts. The ship's carpenters, Robert Gillies and George Berston, fought valiantly to cope with the damage, but continuing storms allowed only slapdash repairs.

Not a man escaped injury. Six of the crew suffered broken arms and cracked ribs. Others had bruises, cuts and sprains. All were drenched to the bone. Miraculously, no one was washed overboard. Unable to cook anything for days at a time, starvation threatened the bedraggled crew.

More than 180 days after leaving Antwerp, a battered *City of Florence* dragged into San Francisco Bay. "Something closely akin to a wreck was towed through the Golden Gate after dark. She had what looked like board fences in half a dozen places. Much of her rigging was worn and spliced," a local newspaper reported. "Even in the inky darkness that prevailed, the few people who boarded her could read the story of havoc by gale and sea."

Captain William Leask commanded the *City of Florence* for half of her life. An experienced skipper, he rounded treacherous Cape Horn forty-two times. *Pat Long.*

On another voyage, the *City of Florence* was sailing in thick fog, sounding her foghorn. The crew thought they heard another foghorn, dead ahead. Through the mist, it appeared as if a ship was on the horizon, showing no sign of changing course. When the lookout called Captain Leask to the deck, he realized that the sound was an echo coming from an iceberg straight ahead and narrowly averted a collision.

In 1899, Captain Leask was forced to retire from the sea. Bashed in the head with a marlin spike by a steward he caught stealing liquor, his health failed. As he left the deck of the ship for the last time, the captain lamented, "Poor old *Florence*, it won't be long now." Captain Leask died of a brain tumor at age fifty-one in 1902, having lived to see his prophecy come true.

HARD ROWING

On her last voyage, the *City of Florence* sailed from Cardiff with twenty-eight officers and crew and a cargo of coal. After discharging the freight at Callao on Peru's western coast, she journeyed eight hundred miles south to load miter at Iquique in northern Chile. Miter, also known as niter or saltpeter, is a critical component of gunpowder. Valued at $60,000, the 1,800-ton payload was consigned to Balfour, Guthrie & Company of San Francisco, the shipping agent for cargo carried by the luckless *Rydal Hall*.

Despite a gale, during which Chief Officer Alexander Fyfe suffered a broken arm, the run north to the California coast was made in good time. On March 19, 1900, the weather was clear, and Captain George E. Stone was able to take good observations until four o'clock that afternoon. Five hours later, after darkness fell, it settled into an eerie calm. "There was a haze on the water that would have fooled the devil himself," lookout Dick McKeever shivered. "It was a thin kind of film that one minute would make you think there was fog, and the next make you rub your eyes to wonder whether you saw anything or not."

Surprised that he hadn't picked up the Farallon Islands light, Captain Stone ordered Third Officer William Thompson aloft for a sighting. "I went aloft and saw the breakers. I got to the deck in a hurry and reported to the captain," Thompson declared. "When he sent me aloft again to make sure, I heard the cry, 'Breakers Ahead.' Almost before I got to the deck again, the ship struck."

The *City of Florence* slammed into the rocks at Half Moon Bay, caromed off, hit again and held fast. Immediately, six feet of water rushed into the hold. The whole bottom was nearly torn out of the ship. "Judging from the sound, she must have gone on a rock but slipped off into deep water again. I thought the ship would go down," a dismayed Captain Stone said later. "I ordered the crew to the pumps. We might as well have tried to pump out the ocean. In about two minutes, ten feet of water was in the hold, and she had taken on a decided list."

With no hope for the ship, the captain ordered the boats lowered. He and eighteen of the crew occupied one lifeboat, while another held Second Mate Inold and the remaining eight crewmen. "Everything was afloat in the cabin so the officers could not save anything. The men secured their effects and got them into the boats," Captain Stone reported. "After getting away from the ship's side, we found ourselves in a sea of breakers. We were surrounded by them and every moment we were in danger of being engulfed. After some very hard rowing, we got clear."

VERY MUCH ASEA

By morning, the *City of Florence* had vanished. The survivors rowed north, assuming that they were south of San Francisco. At midday, the hapless group had seen nothing to indicate that they were anywhere near the Golden Gate. Captain Stone had been to this coast only once before, twenty-seven years before. With his charts still aboard the sunken ship, the befuddled captain felt very much asea. Having come to the conclusion that they must be north of San Francisco, he ordered the crew to row south.

Despite his unfamiliarity with the local coastline, Captain Stone received praise for his poise during the crisis. "The captain was wonderfully cool and collected throughout," Third Officer Thompson acknowledged. "He gave the order to lower the boats when every chance of saving the ship was gone. We all had a close call, and it was wonderful that there was not a mishap."

Luckily, the steamer *Bonita*, bound for Santa Cruz, overtook the floundering bunch about ten miles out to sea. Part of the prominent Pacific

ANOTHER STOUT SHIP LAYS HER BONES ON MONTARA REEF.

1st MATE FYFE AND PART OF HIS

TOWED IN BY THE RELIEF

City of Florence Goes on the Rocks and Is Lost.

Captain Stone Was Away Out of His Proper Course.

Crew of Twenty-seven Comes Safely to This City in the Lost Vessel's Boats.

In 1900, the *City of Florence* slammed into the rocks at Half Moon Bay. Newspaper headlines told of her demise. *From the* San Francisco Chronicle.

Coast Steamship Company's fleet, the *Bonita* was a 180-foot wooden steamer built in 1881 for general cargo and as a passenger carrier. Charles G. Jaeger, a passenger aboard the *Bonita*, explained, "The attention of the crew was attracted by a man in a boat waving a red shirt as a signal of distress."

Captain Nicholson, the steamer's skipper, gave Captain Stone their position and invited the crew aboard. Surprisingly, the invitation was declined. "I wanted to get to San Francisco and decided to come on," a dogged Captain Stone admitted. "We had nothing to eat or drink in our boats, so Capt. Nicholson gave us a three day supply of food and water. Boy, I can tell you it tasted good. That put fresh heart in everybody."

The men were making fair headway back to the north when the tug *Alert*, sent to the rescue skippered by Captain Joe Trewren, intercepted them and brought them safely to port. "The only reason I can give for the loss of my ship is that there must have been a strong current of which I was unaware," Captain Stone shrugged. "The ship was at least twenty miles out of her course when she struck."

In a fitting tribute to a timeworn, Clydebuilt ship, seaman McKeever said gratefully, "It's a mystery to me how the old ship floated as long as she did. She is now over thirty years old, and in those days, they put the proper kind of material into a vessel. Had we been on one of the new-fangled clippers, not a man of us would have been left to tell the tale."

AFTERMATH

The beach where the *City of Florence* wrecked was cluttered with broken masts and spars. According to one newspaper report, "The salvers who went from San Francisco left the wreck to the mercy of the beach combers, finding the sea had left nothing of value to them."

Local residents scoured the shoreline, but not a vestige of the iron vessel's cargo appeared. None of the ship's official papers survived. Only a page from the ship's log book dated 1868 washed ashore, along with two live hogs, which were taken in by a local farmer.

An inquiry into the incident by a Naval Court was held at the British Consulate-General in San Francisco. The court attached no blame to any of the mates or crew of the *City of Florence*. However, it placed responsibility squarely on Captain Stone. The court ruled that "the master of the vessel committed an error in judgement in not pressing on until sunset instead of shortening sail at 4:00 p.m. He would have given himself an opportunity of seeing the mountainous country beyond the Farallon Islands in daylight."

In addition, the court found that by not altering his course for the night, Captain Stone neglected precautions that would have kept the ship out of danger. "By relying on his chronometer, we consider that he was over-confident as to his position. The loss of the ship would not have occurred if he had taken soundings."

As a result of the court's findings, Captain Stone's certificate as master mariner was suspended for six months. It is not known whether he ever boarded a ship again.

CHAPTER 8

MORTALLY WOUNDED

RODERICK DHU, APRIL 25, 1909

Alegendary ship with a mythical name came to a heartbreaking end on the shores of Point Pinos on April 25, 1909. The *Roderick Dhu* (aka *Rhoderick Dhu*) was christened for a fictional Scottish chieftain created by novelist Sir Walter Scott. Her quests were as diverse as the captains who walked her decks.

BEAUTIFUL IRON CLIPPER

Her life at sea was as epic as her name. The *Rhoderick Dhu* entered the world as one of five magnificent iron sailing ships custom-built for the elite Waverly line of Williamson, Milligan & Company of Liverpool, England. Each ship was named for a character in Sir Walter Scott's "Waverly" series: *Ivanhoe*, *Roderick Dhu*, *Lammermoor*, *Cedric the Saxon* and *Kenilworth*. Carrying lavish decorations of scenes and portraits from the novels, the vessels were widely considered among "the most beautiful iron clippers that ever left the ways."

The Waverly line's history was filled with prestige and distinction. John Williamson, a merchant and the company's primary owner, was later chairman of the Standard Marine Insurance Company and a director of the famous Cunard Steamship Company. Many fine officers apprenticed aboard Waverly vessels, including Arthur Henry Rostron. As captain of the *Carpathia* in 1912, he would rescue survivors of the ill-fated *Titanic*.

Launched in 1873, the *Rhoderick Dhu* was a magnificent iron sailing ship named for a character in Sir Walter Scott's novels. *From the San Francisco Call.*

Launched in December 1873, the *Rhoderick Dhu* was 457 feet long and 40 feet wide, measured 1,534 tons and was valued at $140,000. She was fashioned by the illustrious Mounsey & Foster at Sunderland, England. The business had its beginnings in the 1860s when John Haswell established a shipbuilding yard to construct coastal brigs and schooners. Part of the yard was taken over in 1870 by the partnership of Iliff & Mounsey. When Iliff retired three years later, the firm became Mounsey & Foster.

The enterprise specialized in producing small iron sailing ships and steamships. It also made a limited number of vessels like the *Rhoderick Dhu* that became famed among the medium clippers of the period. Each was crafted to accommodate emigrants below decks as well as passengers in upper-deck cabins. According to one sailing expert, "All had a good turn of speed and were powerful ships which would stand unlimited driving."

In the 1870s and 1880s, there was such a host of first-class iron clipper ships making fast passages that it required a real racing skipper to showcase a specific vessel. A ship would spring into prominence for a few voyages and then, at the change of skippers, drop almost out of sight. Historian and sailing captain Peter Johnson observed, "Where so many ships were about equal in their sailing qualities, a particular ship needed to be either especially lucky in her winds or in her master if she was to be numbered among the record breakers."

VARIABLE WINDS

The *Rhoderick Dhu*'s performance received greater publicity in the 1890s than during the 1870s or 1880s. Her first few passages were to Melbourne, Australia, with emigrants. Then, for some years she became a frequent visitor to India's Bay of Bengal, the largest bay in the world. Later, the California grain trade gave her the most employment.

Her first master was Captain Robert Calvert, who steered her on her initial voyage to San Francisco in 1875. By 1882, she was also making cargo runs from Sydney, Australia, to London, England, carrying merchandise such as wool, tallow, leather, cotton, copra, meats, antimony ore, hides and shale. For most of the 1880s, the *Rhoderick Dhu* was commanded by Captain Robert Laurie Boldchild. Born into a noted English seafaring family, he spent his early sailing days with the famous Loch Line trading to Australia. Established in Glasgow in the late 1860s, the Loch Line was a fleet of iron clipper ships named after lochs or lakes in Scotland.

Unfortunately, the Loch Line's reputation was one of misfortune. Seventeen of the twenty-five vessels bearing the *Loch* name sank in accidents, disappeared or were wrecked or torpedoed in oceans and ports around the globe. As chief officer on the bark *Loch Earn*, Captain Boldchild survived a disastrous collision with the French iron steamship *Ville du Havre* in 1873. While the 85 passengers and crew of the *Loch Earn* survived, the steamer was lost in twelve minutes, along with 226 lives.

Captain Boldchild experienced a series of other adventures while at the helm of the *Rhoderick Dhu*. In September 1882, while on a voyage from London to Sydney, a severe gale swamped the ship, yet he skillfully brought the ship to port. "With some violence in the course of the storm, the topsail was blown away and damage done to the port bulwarks," the captain said simply. "It became necessary to work as well as possible against variable winds."

While on a journey through the Dutch East Indies in January 1884, Captain Boldchild reported that the *Rhoderick Dhu* was "passing through large quantities of pumice." The strange navigational hazard was a result of the eruption of the Krakatoa volcano on August 26–27, 1883. The volcano collapsed in a chain of enormous explosions, destroying much of the island and killing more than thirty-six thousand people. For months after the eruption, volcanic dust hung in the air and chunks of the buoyant volcanic rock littered the sea.

One of Captain Boldchild's best passages was eighty-eight days from Liverpool, England, to Calcutta, India, in 1888. When he passed away at age sixty-three in 1909, he was hailed as "a fine old type of British shipmaster."

SWEPT AWAY

On December 8, 1891, the *Rhoderick Dhu* left Liverpool for San Francisco under a new skipper, Captain P.S. Howe. Two other ships, the *Anaurus* and the *Otterpool*, departed for the same destination the day before. Naturally, this led to a great deal of betting in Liverpool on the result of the race between the three vessels. The *Rhoderick Dhu* proved her quality by beating the *Otterpool* by eleven days and the *Anaurus* by thirty-two days.

Three months later, she received a charter to load grain for Hull, England. Located along England's northeastern coast, Hull was an early haven of shipping and trading. Between Cape Horn and the Falkland Islands, the *Rhoderick Dhu* was delayed by huge masses of ice. For three days, Captain Howe picked his way down a narrow water lane between immense bergs. At one time, it was feared that the ship would be trapped amid sheer ice cliffs jutting up to one thousand feet. However, the *Rhoderick Dhu* managed to keep clear and reached Hull in December 1892.

In 1893, the *Rhoderick Dhu* arrived at San Francisco on June 24, having made the passage in 113 days from Dungeness, England. In 1895, she made her last passage around Cape Horn, leaving Liverpool at the end of the summer. Sadly, the voyage was marred by a fatal accident.

On October 30, the ship encountered severe weather and seas off the cape for several days. Her cargo shifted, causing her to list. Second Officer Gerald Scott Coney was on deck directing his watch when huge waves swept the vessel from stem to stern. "He lost his footing, was thrown down, plunged into the boiling ocean and washed under the vessel," one of the crew recalled. "It was evident that he had been badly hurt and probably stunned, as he made no attempt to reach the lines and lifebelts thrown to him. One was thrown almost over his head, but the poor fellow did not see it."

As the crew began to launch a lifeboat, Officer Coney took hold of a lifebuoy that was floating near him. "Words of encouragement were shouted to him, but a heavy wave washed over the gallant young fellow and almost submerged the ship. When the waters subsided, he was nowhere to be seen," the *Liverpool Daily Post* reported. "He was a handsome and manly young fellow and in every respect an ideal sailor. He had a brilliant future ahead of him."

The accident cast a gloom over the entire ship. Just twenty years old, Officer Coney had apprenticed on the *Rhoderick Dhu* and learned his seamanship skills from Captain Howe. In the process, the two became close friends. According to one account, "The captain was very much grieved over the fatality."

"WELL KEPT UP"

The *Rhoderick Dhu* was purchased in 1896 by Captain William E. Matson, who dropped the *h* from her name. Born in Sweden in 1849, Matson was orphaned in childhood and took to the sea at age ten as a "handyboy." Arriving in San Francisco around 1867, he began sailing in San Francisco Bay and Northern California rivers. Matson's life changed when he became acquainted with sugar tycoon J.D. Spreckels, who asked him to serve as skipper on one of the family yachts.

Spreckels assisted Matson in obtaining his first ship in 1882. Matson sailed his three-masted schooner from San Francisco to Hilo, Hawaii, carrying three hundred tons of food, sugar, plantation supplies and general merchandise. The voyage was the birth of the Matson Navigation Company and a long association with the islands.

Matson employed the *Roderick Dhu* in the Hawaiian sugar trade. For years, she kept up a steady, almost monotonous pace carrying freight to Hilo. Trade papers noted, "Although well on in years, she was still one of the handsomest ships on the Pacific coast, and frequently carried passengers to the islands, being both well sailed and well kept up."

On January 29, 1898, under the command of Captain Charles Rock, she arrived at Hilo, just 9

Captain William E. Matson purchased the *Rhoderick Dhu* in 1896. He dropped the *h* from the ship's name. *Hawaii History.*

days from San Francisco, beating a recent record set by the *Henry B. Hyde* between San Francisco and Honolulu. It was quite a feat for the time, given that the *Henry B. Hyde* set several sailing records in the late 1890s. On one occasion, she made the trip from San Francisco to Liverpool in a brisk 102 days. On another voyage, she set the record for the fastest trip from New York to San Francisco to England and back to New York.

Later that year, Captain Rock retired from the sea and turned to farming. For nearly fifty years, he had been a seaman. For more than half of that, he sailed in and out of the Golden Gate as master of San Francisco–owned vessels. "He now thinks he's entitled to a rest," the *San Francisco Call* commented. "Although he has taken to farming, Capt. Rock will not turn his back altogether on the sea. He still retains his interests in at least a dozen vessels."

OCEAN WAIFS

Captain Rock was succeeded by Captain Peter Johnson. Born in 1863, Johnson answered the call of the sea at age fourteen, shipping out as a cook on a Swedish sailing vessel. He joined the crew of the full-rigged American ship *Great Republic*, then the largest ship afloat, traveling with it to Boston, Massachusetts. For several years, Johnson sailed the seven seas, touching every large port in the world. He wrote, "I can't remember the day when I wasn't in or around ships."

Johnson also served on the infamous *T.F. Oakes* between San Francisco and Hull, England, in 1884. One of only three large full-rigged iron ships ever built in the United States, the *T.F. Oakes* went on to become one of the most notorious ships to ever sail. During the voyage, a baby was born. "Naturally, I can't remember anything about the trip, but my mother told me later that it was a rough one," Mrs. C.J. Hicks recalled. "The ship got into some jam or other and never made a trip after without some jinx."

Soon after, Johnson met William E. Matson and spent the rest of his career in Matson's employ. He set a breezy pace on the *Roderick Dhu*, making one trip from San Francisco to Hilo in nine and a half days when other vessels were averaging twenty. Although Captain Johnson soon gained a reputation as "one of the ablest of the present generation of ship masters," he credited his ship and crew for much of the success. "The *Roderick Dhu* was a wonderful ship," he declared. "She was a fast sailer and I had good officers, so we made good time."

During two of his voyages, the captain observed unusual instances of birds taking refuge on the *Roderick Dhu*. In May or June 1897, a brown hawk boarded about two hundred miles outbound from Hilo and stayed for the duration of the trip to California. The bird made excursions to prey for food but always returned to its same perch on the ship.

In October 1900, some five hundred miles from the Hawaiian Islands, an owl alighted in the *Roderick Dhu*'s rigging. The bird was so fatigued that it was easily caught by hand and placed in a coop. Regrettably, the owl refused to eat and died within a week. No doubt the little waif was given a proper burial at sea.

An Omen

As Matson expanded his fleet, he introduced some dramatic maritime innovations to some of his vessels. The first Matson steamship, the *Enterprise*, was the first offshore ship in the Pacific to burn oil instead of coal. In 1900, the *Roderick Dhu* was the first ship to be fitted with electricity and a cold storage plant. "He could see farther than any man I ever met," Johnson said of Matson. "I admired him tremendously for it."

The *Roderick Dhu* continued along in the thriving Hawaii trade, hauling her usual cargo as well as hefty equipment to build new sugar mills. In 1905, she was acquired by the Associated Oil Company when it purchased Matson's Pacific Oil & Transportation Company. Matson's fleet of vessels and fuel oil tanks on San Francisco Bay formed the nucleus of Associated Oil's new marine transportation department. The total carrying capacity of this original fleet—which consisted of the *Roderick Dhu*, *Marion Chilcott*, *Rosecrans*, *Santiago*, *Monterey* and *Falls of Clyde*—was about eighty thousand barrels.

The *Roderick Dhu* faced a major transition when her owners converted her to a barge for carrying bulk oil. She settled down to a peaceful life, being towed by various tugs back and forth between San Francisco and Southern California. All was serene until the morning of January 21, 1909. Tied up at the Redondo Beach Wharf near Los Angeles, heavy seas proved too much for the *Roderick Dhu*'s mooring lines. In minutes, she was pitched ashore. Her skipper, Captain W.Z. Haskins, attributed the episode to the "peril of the sea." The captain would later create active shipbuilding and lumber enterprises that served ports in the Pacific Northwest.

A wharf crew, under the direction of Superintendent M.T. Maddex, passed a line to the stranded vessel, attached it to the switch engine of a

The *Roderick Dhu* wrecked near Point Pinos in 1909. Pinned on the rocks, she disintegrated into a watery grave. *Pacific Grove Museum of Natural History*.

locomotive and attempted to pull the ship off the sand. The first attempt failed when the line parted. A second line was secured on the barge, this time attached to her stern. The *Roderick Dhu* was re-floated successfully, "none the worse for her experience." The tug *Navigator* took over, towing the barge and her cargo on to San Francisco.

Her return trip was equally eventful. Heavily laden with oil, the *Roderick Dhu* was attempting to leave San Francisco on January 23 when she encountered a furious gale. A huge wave swept over the stern, parting the tow line, smashing the ship's wheel and carrying two seamen overboard. The tug *Hercules* was sent to secure another hawser, while the revenue cutter *McCulloch* took the ship's officers and crew aboard. The sailors, Charles Verdich and John Maher, were retrieved from the sea. Badly injured, they were taken to the harbor hospital for emergency treatment. The journey was an omen of more terrible things to come.

EMBATTLED CHIEFTAIN

For nearly three more months, the *Roderick Dhu* continued transporting oil on the California coast. In the early morning hours of April 25, 1909, the barge was being towed by the 204-ton tug *Relief*. The tug's master, Captain Marshall, thought that he was guiding the vessels toward the entrance to Monterey Bay when he mistakenly entered a rocky inlet. Realizing his error, the skipper swung the tug around and headed for open sea.

Unluckily, the towing cables snapped, and having no power of her own, the *Roderick Dhu* drove onto the rocks. As her iron hull ground to a halt, Captain Haskins ordered the anchors dropped to prevent her from being carried farther inshore. The skipper and his crew made their way safely off the wreck and quickly established a camp on the beach to prevent piracy. From Point Pinos, light keeper Emily Fish reported, "Partly clear, drifting fog. The *Roderick Dhu* went ashore at high tide a mile and a quarter south of the lighthouse."

From San Francisco, Associated Oil Company dispatched the 155-ton tug *Defiance* to aid the *Relief* in a rescue attempt. Together, the two tugs attempted to haul the barge from the rocks during the incoming high tide. Unfortunately, the combined horsepower of the tugs only caused the *Roderick Dhu* to list toward the breakers. The helpless vessel sat broadside to the beach with rocks piercing her hull. Just like the embattled chieftain for whom she was named, the *Roderick Dhu* lay mortally wounded.

In the ensuing days, Associated Oil made several dogged attempts to re-float the damaged vessel. The steamer *Greenwood* arrived with wrecking apparatus, and the revenue cutter *McCullough* brought lifesaving equipment. With the *Roderick Dhu* valued at $175,000, a final effort was made to keep her intact. Divers attempted repairs, but these, too, proved unsuccessful. As a last resort, holes were cut in the side of the hull to extract cargo, machinery and anything else of use.

Meanwhile, Captain Norman Nelson of the Golden Gate Life-Saving Station arrived. Although Captain Nelson had been station chief for only a year, he and his intrepid crew had participated in many notable rescues and were lauded often for their courage and attention to duty. "We are paid by Uncle Sam to be life-savers," Captain Nelson asserted. "That means we must save lives. I have taught the men that the first thing to consider, in all cases, is the saving of life."

Once satisfied that no lives were in danger, the captain and his men gathered food and cooking equipment from the wreck for the stranded survivors. When Captain Nelson learned that the shipwrecked mariners had left their clothing and personal property aboard, he returned again. He also ran lines from the *Roderick Dhu* to the beach so those ashore could reach the vessel as necessary in perfect safety.

Captain Norman Nelson and the crew of the Golden Gate Life-Saving Station aided stranded survivors of the *Roderick Dhu*. *From the* Overland Monthly.

Credited with being the "hero of the wreck," Captain Nelson appropriated a souvenir for the lifesaving station: the ship's figurehead. Today, it resides at the San Francisco Maritime Museum. What remained of the *Roderick Dhu* was abandoned and gradually disintegrated under the pounding surf. According to one local writer, "Rocks and winds and seas collapsed the big steel hull of the *Roderick Dhu* who joined her predecessors in their watery graves."

CHAPTER 9

IMMERSED IN MISFORTUNES

USS *H-3*, JUNE 29, 1915

A small navy submarine, the USS *H-3* experienced more than her share of misadventures. Her grounding at Point Sur on June 29, 1915, was only one of many hardships she would endure. Her most memorable misfortune involved the loss of the multimillion-dollar navy cruiser *Milwaukee* in 1917.

UNDERWATER BOATS

The concept of an underwater boat has captivated people for centuries. Ancient Egyptian, Greek and Islamic images depict divers swimming underwater breathing through hollow reeds. Primitive diving bells are illustrated, too—even one made of glass.

The first published description of a submersible craft came in 1580 from William Bourne, an English innkeeper and amateur scientist. He wrote, "It is possible to make a ship or boat that may go under the water unto the bottom, and so to come up again at your pleasure. It would swim when you would and sink when you list."

Dutchman Cornelius J. Drebble, the "court inventor" for James I of England, is credited with building the first working submarine in 1623. According to all accounts, this was a wood-encased rowboat propelled by twelve oarsmen. Apparently, the vessel completed a submerged journey down London's Thames River at a depth of about fifteen feet. Other versions of submersibles continued to appear through the 1700s.

The first military submarine, the *Turtle*, was constructed in 1776 during the American Revolutionary War. The vessel was a hand-powered, egg-shaped device designed by David Bushnell to accommodate a single man. She was the first submarine capable of independent underwater operation and movement, as well as the first to use propellers for propulsion.

Although the *Turtle* didn't serve in the U.S. Navy, she is reputed to be the first submarine to assault an enemy vessel. In the early morning hours of September 7, 1776, operated by Sergeant Ezra Lee, the *Turtle* prepared to strike the British warship HMS *Eagle* in New York Harbor. Lee became disoriented, bobbed to the surface and was spotted by the *Eagle*'s lookout. Startled, Lee beat a hasty retreat and escaped unscathed.

Robert Fulton, an American artist, engineer and inventor living in Paris during the French Revolutionary Wars, offered to construct a submarine to defend France against Britain in 1800. "The mechanical *Nautilus*," he insisted, "flatters me with much hope of being able to annihilate their Navy." He offered to build and operate the device at his own expense and accept payment for each British ship destroyed. Although Fulton made several attempts to attack English ships, most detected him and steered safely from harm's way. Frustrated, Fulton dismantled the vessel and sold it for scrap. Later, he gained fame when he built the first commercial steamboat.

EARLY SUBMARINES

In the 1850s, French émigré and engineer Brutus de Villeroi developed a prototype of a submarine that was perfectly round and shaped like a fish. Newspapers said of his experimental tests, "The result was eminently satisfactory and fully demonstrates the practicability of the invention."

When America's Civil War began, de Villeroi pitched his invention to President Abraham Lincoln. "I propose to you a new arm of war, as formidable as it is economical," he stated. "Submarine navigation, which has been sometimes attempted but as all know without results, owing to want of suitable opportunities, is a problematical thing no more."

In the autumn of 1861, the U.S. Navy asked the noted firm of Neafie & Levy of Philadelphia, Pennsylvania, to construct a small submersible ship based on de Villeroi's design. The ship was about thirty feet long and six to eight feet in diameter. Reports said, "The vessel was made of iron, with the upper part pierced for small circular plates of glass for light, and in it were several water tight compartments."

John Holland developed the prototype for a submarine torpedo boat. In 1900, he built the U.S. Navy's first submarine, the USS *Holland*. *U.S. Navy.*

Dubbed the *Alligator*, the vessel was launched in May 1862 but was never commissioned. Unfortunately, the ship proved cumbersome and saw little action in battle. Less than a year later, the short-lived *Alligator* foundered and sank in a storm off Cape Hatteras, North Carolina.

The Civil War also saw the first submarine to sink her target. The Confederate vessel *H.L. Hunley* was operated by eight men turning a hand crank attached to the propeller shaft. During trial runs, the forty-foot vessel sank twice, killing all aboard, before proving successful. Under cover of darkness on February 16, 1864, the *Hunley* sank the USS *Housatonic*, which was on Union blockade duty in Charleston Harbor. For unknown reasons, the submarine sank soon after. Remarkably, she was recovered in August 2000.

In 1888, the Navy announced a competition to develop a "submarine torpedo boat." The competition called for a boat that could travel for ninety hours at fifteen knots on the surface or eight knots submerged. The vessel had to dive to 150 feet and have a turning ability less than four times its length. John P. Holland, an Irish immigrant and inventor, won the competition but not a contract.

Holland entered and won another Navy competition in 1893, this time receiving a contract. In 1900, the U.S. Navy commissioned its first submarine, the USS *Holland*. "The ship was designed with many of the features common to its modern day descendants," one account noted, "including the teardrop shaped hull and internally re-loadable torpedo tubes."

Tenacity and Hard Work

After launching the *Holland*, the Navy began building other submarines. Between 1900 and 1913, several classes of submarines were completed, sequentially designated as "A" through "H." Each new class of submarine marked an improvement in both quality and performance over previous ones.

Known as the *Garfish* while under construction, the USS *H-3* was commissioned in January 1914. The vessel indeed resembled a needle-nosed fish. She measured 358 tons, was 150 feet long and 16 feet wide and carried a usual complement of twenty-five officers and crew. She was constructed by Moran Brothers, a prominent shipbuilding firm in Seattle, Washington.

Founded in 1882, Moran Brothers was known for its tenacity and hard work. The driving force behind the enterprise was Robert Moran. Born in 1857 in New York City, he left school at the age of fourteen to acquire training as a machinist. In 1875, he migrated to the Pacific coast, going first to San Francisco and then on to Seattle. For a time, he found employment as a steamboat engineer in Puget Sound, British Columbia and Alaska.

Moran saved his earnings and sent for other family members. In 1882, he and his brothers, Peter and William, opened a small machine shop with an initial capital of $1,500. The plant was worth $40,000 when the Great Seattle Fire of June 6, 1889, swept it away. Undeterred, the firm reopened for business ten days later in temporary quarters.

By then, Robert Moran had been elected mayor of Seattle. "His leadership in recovery activities won him a second term," one commentary asserted. "Through the period of his mayoralty, he was instrumental in rebuilding of businesses. His political connections were also very helpful in securing government contracts for his shipbuilding company."

Moran was also a large stockholder in the Seattle Dry Dock & Shipbuilding Company, a shipyard and marine railway that adjoined the Moran Brothers foundry and machine shops. By 1891, a well-equipped dry dock to repair and build ships had been completed. The company prospered, producing paddlewheel riverboats during the Klondike Gold Rush of 1897. In 1902, the firm became Seattle's largest employer when it won a naval contract to build the battleship USS *Nebraska*. The vessel became the flagship of the U.S. Navy's "Great White Fleet," sent around the world by President Theodore Roosevelt to demonstrate American naval power.

By 1905, the stress of business had taken a toll on Moran's health, and doctors gave him a short time to live. He retreated to Orcas Island in northern Puget Sound, where he built the Moran Mansion. "He began to build his retirement home with the same integrity as one of his ocean going vessels: massive and solid, yet elegant and gracious," one biographer observed. "Free from the pressures of his business, Moran recovered and lived until 1943."

Moran Brothers Company was sold in 1906. The new owners reorganized the business under the name of the Moran Company, which later became the Seattle Construction & Dry Dock Company. In 1911, the firm began building the first of six submarines for the U.S. Navy, including the *H-3*.

SLIGHTLY WORSE FOR WEAR

After a shakedown cruise, the *H-3* was attached to the Pacific Fleet and began patrolling the coast of California and Washington. Hailed as "one of the newer craft," her homeport was at San Pedro in Southern California, the site of the first submarine base on the Pacific coast.

Spirits were high as the *H-3* steamed north from San Diego to participate in San Francisco's Fourth of July naval pageant. Just nine years after the devastating 1906 earthquake, the city was staging the 1915 Panama-Pacific International Exposition, celebrating the opening of the Panama Canal in August 1914 and showing more than 18 million visitors from around the world that it remained "the city that knew how."

On June 29, the mood aboard ship shifted. Struggling through heavy winds and dense fog near Point Sur, the sub's skipper, Lieutenant William F. Newton, lost his bearings. Unwittingly, he ran the ship ashore. Caught on a flat rock amidships, the *H-3* sat with her bow projecting four feet out of the water, listing sharply to starboard. Early reports said, "Owing to the character of the coast line at the point where the submarine is ashore, grave fears are entertained that her predicament may be serious."

The *H-3* experienced more than her share of misadventures. In 1915, she grounded off Point Sur. *U.S. Navy.*

Forest Supervisor Norman Sloane was the first to receive news of the wreck. In the company of two other men, E.A. Abbott and Alden H. Abbott, he hopped into his new Ford automobile and started for Point Sur Lighthouse. "The trip was made over dangerous roads with much personal risk to the venturesome trio," the *Monterey American* exclaimed. "Throughout the trip, the signaling of the fog horn of the wrecked ship could be plainly heard. Answering calls from the ships out at sea could also be heard. These boats do not dare to come in toward the dangerous coast until the fog lifts."

Luckily, Sloane and his colleagues reached the lighthouse safely. Undaunted by the persistent haze, they joined Point Sur's keepers in a small boat and set out toward the grounded submarine. The group made soundings to determine the best channel through which rescuing ships might proceed.

Many feared that the *H-3* was suffering such a pounding on the rocks that there was little hope of saving her. According to one observer, "Time and time again during the eighteen hour battle with giant combers the little craft was lifted and hurled back with smashing force while the crew expected it to go to pieces with each shivering crash."

Fortunately, the *H-3* was in the company of her mother ship, the USS *Cheyenne*, and sister ships, the *H-1* and the *H-2*, when the mishap occurred.

At high tide the following day, the *H-3* was rescued by the *Cheyenne* and hauled into deep water. "When the boat sheered off into deep water, ending the anxiety of the crew, scores of persons on the shore half a mile away cheered lustily," the *San Francisco Chronicle* revealed. "The officers in the conning tower of the submarine waved back a greeting."

The battered sub proved only slightly worse for wear. A partially bent keel and two small leaks caused by sprung plates constituted the only damage. After steaming through the Golden Gate under her own power, the *H-3* docked near the Exposition grounds. Later, Lieutenant Newton gave early morning visitors a practical demonstration of the maneuvering prowess of the submarine by running her up and down the bay and circling the *Cheyenne* and other ships in the vicinity.

Unseemly Experience

Although her encounter with the rocks at Point Sur ended happily, this was not the last of the *H-3*'s mishaps. On January 22, 1916, she ran aground on a San Diego mud flat. Once again she was rescued by the *Cheyenne* and remained undamaged. However, a voyage later the same year resulted in disaster.

On the morning of December 14, accompanied by three other navy vessels, the little sub was approaching Eureka in Northern California. Along with the submarines *H-1* and *H-2* and the tender *Cheyenne*, the *H-3* was assigned "to gather information about future facilities at coast ports for the care of submarines."

The mission would never be completed. Temporarily disabled by a failed engine, the *H-3* crept along a coast cloaked in fog. Her inexperienced skipper, Lieutenant Harry Bogusch, lost his way, and thinking that he saw smoke from the *Cheyenne*, he steered in that direction. The sub struck a sandspit and ran aground at Samoa Beach near the entrance to Humboldt Bay. The smoke, it turned out, was from a nearby mill.

"The ship, a fragile toy caught in the powerful grip of a brutal sea, thrashed convulsively in the churning breakers," one report declared. "Leaking batteries discharged clouds of chlorine gas. The crew, choking from the deadly vapors and pitching about wildly in their iron-clad prison, fought a desperate battle against a blazing inferno in the engine room."

With the *H-3*'s crew helpless in the pounding surf and her companion ships unable to reach her from offshore, the local lifesaving crew began rescue operations. During the afternoon, a Coast Guard surfboat was able

The *H-3* capsized near Eureka, California, in 1916. Rescue attempts resulted in the loss of the multimillion-dollar cruiser USS *Milwaukee. U.S. Navy.*

to carry a line to the stranded submarine. By early evening, the *H-3*'s twenty-seven officers and crew were brought ashore by a breeches buoy—a circular lifebuoy attached to a pair of rubber pants, commonly used by lifesaving crews to extract people from wrecked vessels.

Storm surf pushed the *H-3* high up onto the sandy beach, surrounded by quicksand. At low tide, she was seventy-five feet from the water. Efforts by the *Cheyenne* and the USS *Iroquois* to dislodge her proved fruitless. Both ships returned to the Mare Island Navy Yard in San Francisco while bids were requested from commercial salvage firms.

The bids ranged from $18,000 to $72,000. According to one report, "The government was skeptical about any of the contractors' ability to carry out this work and therefore decided to attempt to salvage the vessel themselves by towing her to sea."

Unwisely, the Navy sent the armored cruiser USS *Milwaukee* to tow the *H-3* from the sand. Built by Union Iron Works in San Francisco, the ship entered naval service in 1906 and was deployed to the Pacific Ocean. Two steel cables two inches in diameter and four thousand feet long were attached to the submarine and to the stern of the *Milwaukee*. On January 13, 1917, after many attempts and the loss of one sailor's life, the *Milwaukee* made one final valiant effort.

Things went awry very quickly. As heavy fog set in, the cruiser drifted into the breakers and smacked hard aground. The pounding surf split open her hull and dismounted most of her machinery. One observer moaned, "The *Milwaukee*, a seven million dollar, four-stack, first class cruiser had come ashore to stay."

Her endangered crew, some 450 men, had to be rescued. Some were brought ashore by breeches buoy and others by boat, averting any loss of life. Within a few days, many of the survivors were sent by train to Mare Island, while others began the task of salvaging equipment from the *Milwaukee*'s wreckage.

In 2019, archaeologists conducted a survey of the exposed wreckage and adjacent sand dunes. They recorded what remains of the *Milwaukee* and its associated salvage camp to see if enough archaeological material remains to warrant further research. Where she sits today is not so much on the sand as under it. Every year, the ship's remnants sink lower and lower. Now, just the tips of a few bulkheads are visible at low tide.

Upon Due Reflection

Upon due reflection, the Navy turned back to the private sector to recover the *H-3*. Officials accepted the $18,000 bid by the Mercer-Fraser lumber company. Instead of attempting to refloat the submarine where she lay, risking the heavy breakers, the firm proposed dragging the *H-3* across the bar and launching her into Humboldt Bay.

Two redwood logs were placed alongside her, and cables were passed underneath and secured to these logs. Smaller timbers were placed inside the cables so that the *H-3* rested in a cradle. A road was constructed across the bar, and the sub was pulled in the cradle. She was re-floated in the quiet waters of Humboldt Bay on July 25. All in all, it was a very unseemly experience. Following repairs, the *H-3* returned to San Pedro, California, where her trials and tribulations continued.

On May 27, 1922, five seamen were injured in an explosion while she was on patrol duty off the Coronado Islands, forty miles from San Diego. The blast occurred in the engine compartment among storage batteries. Fortunately, although the men received burns in fighting a fire that followed the explosion, they were not seriously hurt.

She returned to service, was sent to the Atlantic and was decommissioned in October. In 1931, after nine years laid up at the Philadelphia Navy Yard, the *H-3* was scrapped. Her miseries were over at last.

The *H-3* was salvaged by being placed on giant log rollers and taken overland to Humboldt Bay. After repairs, she was re-floated. *U.S. Navy.*

Despite her troubles, she held a special place in the hearts and minds of her crew. "They weren't just hull numbers, they were our home addresses," submariner Dick Murphy mused. "Now the old neighborhood is torn down and gone, and all that is left are memories."

CHAPTER 10

FIERY SPECTER

BABINDA, MARCH 4, 1923

Although the *Babinda* was designed to support World War I shipping needs, she was destined for other service. Her end came in a fiery blaze at sea near Point Sur on March 4, 1923, despite persistent warning cries from the ship's mascot.

EMERGENCY FLEET

America's growing involvement in World War I began after German submarines relentlessly attacked U.S. merchant ships. On April 2, 1917, President Woodrow Wilson asked Congress to declare war on Germany. One month later, he also requested the formation of the U.S. Shipping Board to oversee the nation's wartime shipping activities.

The board formed an Emergency Fleet Corporation for the "purchase, construction, equipment, lease, charter, maintenance and operation of merchant vessels in the commerce of the United States." It engaged in what was then the greatest construction task ever attempted by a single organization.

"Our country needs ships to carry our boys 'over there' and keep them well supplied with food, clothing and the munitions of war," one production poster declared. "The ships can be completed only as fast as the material and equipment for each ship arrives in the shipyard. If every man does a better day's work every day, the ships can be built faster."

The steamship *Babinda* was a general cargo carrier designed to support World War I shipping needs. *Monterey History and Maritime Museum.*

When America entered the war, the nation's shipbuilders were involved principally in turning out ships for other countries such as Britain, Norway and Australia. Once the Emergency Fleet Corporation was formed, all steel ships under construction of more than 2,500 tons were commandeered to support the country's war efforts.

However, many wooden ships escaped requisitioning, including the three-thousand-ton steamship *Babinda*. The vessel was designed for the Commonwealth Government Line of Steamers in Sydney, Australia, to transport wheat and wool to Europe and America. Her name is said to come from the Aboriginal word *borrabinda*, meaning waterfall or valley of rain.

The *Babinda* was built by the Patterson-MacDonald Shipbuilding Company near Seattle, Washington. The vessel was a general cargo carrier equipped with "the latest cargo handling appliances." She had a length of 268 feet, was 48 feet wide, measured 3,000 tons and had 1,000-horsepower twin engines.

During the war, Patterson-McDonald proved to be the "leading yard from a production standpoint for Australian interests." By the time the *Babinda* was completed in December 1918, war efforts were winding down, and Australia no longer needed the steamer. She was sold in early 1919 to John E. Chilberg, a Seattle merchant and entrepreneur.

TROUBLED TIMES

Born in Iowa in 1867, Chilberg arrived in Seattle, Washington, as a youngster. He began his career working in his father's store, rising to the position of manager. When his father retired in 1888, the business was incorporated as N. Chilberg & Son and was the largest wholesale and retail grocery company in the city.

Following a devastating store fire in 1889, he became engaged as a merchandise broker, dealing in wholesale and retail crockery, glassware, lamps, flour, feed and grain. He also represented the three largest flour mills on the Pacific coast: Starr & Company of San Francisco, C&C Roller Mills of Spokane and Oregon Milling Company of Portland.

"Mr. Chilberg is one of the youngest businessmen in Seattle and has with wonderful perseverance managed to build up his company which was almost completely prostrated by the great fire," *Seattle Illustrated* proclaimed. "He is one of the best and most favorably known businessmen in the city."

In 1892, Chilberg began selling merchandise in Central America, sailing often from San Francisco to Panama. During a voyage in 1895, the steamship *Colima* foundered in heavy seas off the coast of Mexico. Chilberg was among the passengers aboard.

Thrown into the water with splintered timbers, he drifted amid the floating debris before encountering four other men clinging to a raft. Three hours later, they were washed ashore carrying few personal possessions. "We were battered, bruised and half naked," Chilberg recalled. "The hands of my poor little watch stand just as they stopped when I took my plunge off the sinking *Colima*."

"The crystal was broken by a stick of lumber striking me in the side, almost knocking me senseless, but I kept a grip on a piece of the deckhouse and I am alive," he continued. "That watch, rusted and battered, is the most valuable timepiece in the world to me. It reminds me and always will record an hour the most horrible in all my life."

As one of only 31 survivors, Chilberg had been fortunate. Drowned in the tragic wreck were 218 other passengers and members of the crew.

Between 1897 and 1905, Chilberg operated steamers out of Alaska, held interests in the Pioneer Mining Company and the Miners and Merchants Bank of Nome and became president of the Scandinavian-American Bank. He also organized the Century Company, constructed the first fireproof office building in Seattle and served as president of the Alaska-Yukon Pacific Exposition of 1909.

After the *Babinda* was completed in 1918, she was sold to John Chilberg (middle right), a Seattle merchant and entrepreneur. *From* Seattle Illustrated.

Troubled times came in 1920 when the Scandinavian-American Bank collapsed. Chilberg was accused of borrowing large sums from the bank without the directors' approval. Although he was acquitted of any wrongdoing, he withdrew from civic affairs and moved to Southern California.

FUNERAL PYRE

The *Babinda* was repossessed by the Australian government and sold to the newly formed Pacific Motorship Company. In 1922, she was passed on to the Ocean Motorship Company of San Francisco and Portland and operated by the Pacific Steamship Company. The enterprise was created in 1916 when the Pacific Coast Steamship Company merged with the Pacific-Alaska Navigation Company.

"The consolidation made the new company virtually supreme in the coastwise service between Puget Sound and California ports," colleagues acknowledged, "and rivaled the Alaska Steamship Company in the trade between Seattle and Alaska." The firm operated both passenger and cargo vessels until 1933, when it reorganized as Pacific Steamship Lines.

The *Babinda* continued to carry assorted cargo and merchandise, including pulp and paper products. Sadly, the final voyage of the stalwart steamer was destined to be a lonely one. Making her usual run between San Pedro and San Francisco, the ship burst into flames near Santa Cruz. Apparently, the fire started in the engine room during the early morning hours of March 3, 1923. A similar mishap had occurred within the past year.

Aboard the *Babinda* were twenty-three officers and crew. On watch was Second Engineer Harry Hillstad. "He stopped the engines and with other members of the crew tried to put out the blaze," one account relayed, "but the fire spread rapidly and in a few minutes the entire engine room was enveloped in flames."

Hillstad rushed to the bridge, where Captain W.H. Maland radioed an SOS. The captain and his crew of twenty continued to battle the inferno for more than an hour, but the conflagration only spread. "The smoke was stifling, the heat intense," one report declared. "Yet, they fought on. Slowly, the blaze threatened the fuel tanks. It looked as if the crew were doomed."

Fortunately, a McCormick Steamship Company passenger ship, the *Celilo*, happened to be in the area. Begun in 1901 to build and operate wooden steam schooners, the McCormick Steamship Company was a subsidiary of the Charles R. McCormick Lumber Company. By 1916, the firm's vessels were serving all major ports on the Pacific coast. "Here are ever-to-be-remembered hours of enchantment and pleasure as your ship glides through the great Pacific," a promotional brochure read. "All that you could ask for is offered on a finely appointed McCormick steamship."

On this voyage, the *Celilo*'s passengers received more than the usual entertainment when Captain G.H. Swanson responded to the *Babinda*'s SOS. "It looks as if we can't keep the fire from the fuel tanks," Captain Maland mega-phoned from the bridge of his sweltering vessel. "We are going to leave the ship in small boats." At that time, the *Babinda* was enveloped in a dense cloud of black smoke through which a fireball rose, lighting the water. Captain Swanson and his crew fought through the blistering heat, rescuing the desperate survivors.

Witnessing the scene were a number of local fishermen. Although many sent their boats to help, the *Babinda* was ablaze from stem to stern. Tongues of fire leaped fifty to sixty feet above the deck, sending a great pyramid of smoke and flames into the sky. "The *Babinda* is doomed," one skipper observed. "We were about a hundred yards from her. She's burning fore and aft fiercely, and just before we started back the bridge was falling."

Smoldering like a Viking funeral pyre, the *Babinda* continued her desolate journey, drifting south with the wind and current. More than twenty-four hours later, she reached the waters of Point Sur, nearly forty miles from where she'd been abandoned. Joining the decaying hulks of other wrecks, the *Babinda*'s scorched remains slipped beneath the sea at 7:10 a.m. on March 4, 1923. The loss was estimated to be $200,000.

STANDING BY

At the time the forlorn ship sank, several vessels, including the Red Stack tug *Sea Lion*, were standing by. Built in 1884, the iron-hulled tug was 150 feet in length, carried a one-thousand-horsepower steam engine and was noted for "performing excellent work." Tugs are vastly misunderstood. These sturdy, steadfast boats are the heart of the harbor. They are the soul of ships, escorting them to safe port or rescuing them from harm. In this case, it was hoped that something could be retrieved. Captain William J. Darragh of the *Sea Lion* revealed that before sinking, the *Babinda* "was a mass of flames from stem to stern and that there was no chance to salvage any part of the ill-fated craft."

Thomas B. Crowley launched the famous "Red Stack Fleet," known far and wide by the bright markings on the stacks of the vessels. He began the enterprise with eighty dollars, purchasing an eighteen-foot classic Whitehall rowboat to provide transportation of personnel and stores to ships anchored on San Francisco Bay. In his first decade of business, he established the philosophy of reinvesting his profits into the firm, continually looking to make improvements in equipment and methodology. Soon, the one Whitehall was joined by two others serving the bay twenty-four hours a day. In the mid-1890s, the business was incorporated under the name Thomas Crowley and Brothers.

Crowley purchased his first thirty-six-foot motor launch vessel shortly followed by a forty-five-foot vessel and then a twenty-eight-footer. Within a few years, services broadened to include bay towing and ship-assist services. He continued to build new or buy used gasoline launches, expanding both the fleet and the type of work the company could perform. The company also acquired and operated small barges to transport steel to Oakland and barrels of oil, ice and other supplies to ships in the bay.

In the 1920s, Crowley expanded services north into Washington's Puget Sound and south into Los Angeles Harbor. In 1937, he entered into a new partnership with Smith Rice Derrick Barges Inc., which provided dredging, marine construction and other services at the Los Angeles Harbor, as well as Long Beach and San Diego. When Thomas Crowley passed away in 1970, the *San Francisco Chronicle* wrote, "He began his life as a Whitehaller and ended up controlling most of the tugs between San Diego and Alaska."

UNHEEDED WARNING

As the fiery ghost ship sank, bystander Tom Majors commented, "The flare of the blaze resembled a huge sunset." With the *Babinda* went a special member of the crew named Jerry. He was the only one who had an inkling of trouble. Sadly, he proved to be a martyr whose warning went unheeded. He was the ship's mascot, a black cat of hermit-like habits.

Dogs and cats were common aboard ships as mascots. Cats have been carried on ships for many reasons, most importantly to control rodents, which could cause damage to ropes, woodwork and wiring. These pests could threaten ships' stores, devour crews' foodstuffs and cause economic damage to cargo such as grain. Rodents could also be a source of disease for ships that were at sea for long periods.

SHIP'S MASCOT TRIES TO WARN CREW OF PERIL

Babinda's Black Cat Makes Unheeded Appeals and Perishes in Fire

HELD WILD NIGHT ORGY

Officers and Men Put Pet Out of Quarters Before Flames Discovered

Cries of peril from the *Babinda's* mascot, a black cat named Jerry, went unheeded. Sadly, Jerry perished with the ship. *From the* San Francisco Chronicle.

Although in many cultures a black cat symbolizes bad luck or misfortune, sailors thought otherwise. Cats were believed to have miraculous powers that brought good luck and protected ships from dangerous weather. In addition, cats offered companionship and a sense of home, security and camaraderie to sailors away from home.

Normally, Jerry was content to spend his days in the foc'sle, never venturing beyond the Number One hatch. "He never cried and there were some who never knew of his existence," one crew member reminisced. "However, on the night before the fire, Jerry was unusually restless and paced the deck whining and mewing. No one paid any attention."

When Captain Maland retired at 9:30 p.m., the cat's agitation increased. Jerry dashed into the skipper's cabin, jumped on his bunk and began to howl. The captain put him out, but the cat ran into the officers' quarters, where he repeated his performance.

Put out of the officers' quarters, Jerry spent the rest of the night running around the ship, caterwauling and generally annoying the crew. Surprisingly, no one thought to attach significance to his odd behavior. When the fire broke out at 3:45 a.m., Jerry disappeared. In the turmoil, he was forgotten.

"And now Jerry is dead, mourned by those members of the crew who had the privilege of knowing him," a survivor grieved. "He tried his frantic best to warn the officers and crew of the impending disaster."

CHAPTER 11

"WE ARE STRUCK!"

SAN JUAN, AUGUST 29, 1929

At midnight on August 29, 1929, the passenger steamship *San Juan* was struck by the oil tanker *S.C.T. Dodd* in the fog-obscured waters of Pigeon Point. It was the Coastside's worst maritime tragedy.

LEADING SHIPBUILDER

The steamship *San Juan* splashed into the water in 1882, launching what would become a legendary career. She was fashioned by the distinguished John Roach at Chester, Pennsylvania. Born in Ireland in 1815, Roach rose from humble origins to create one of the most prestigious shipbuilding empires in America.

Roach left home at the age of sixteen and secured a job at the Allaire Iron Works in Howell, New Jersey. Allaire was one of the world's first companies dedicated to the development of the marine steam engine. Initially, Roach worked as a laborer at twenty-five cents per day, collecting bricks and conveying them by wheelbarrow to building sites around the property. Eager to do more, he sought the trade of an iron moulder.

The firm's proprietor, James P. Allaire, charged an apprentice fee of sixty dollars but was so impressed by Roach's dedication that he waived payment. Other workers were resentful and did little to enhance Roach's skills. When Allaire became aware of the situation, he gathered the tradesmen together. "You see this boy. It is my wish that he should learn the trade," Allaire demanded. "See to it that my wishes are not further disregarded."

The steamship *San Juan* was launched in 1882. She was built by the distinguished John Roach at Chester, Pennsylvania. *San Mateo County History Museum.*

Roach's fellow workers complied, and he became a highly skilled craftsman. Later, he was transferred to the company's engine building plant in New York City. During his twelve years at the plant, Roach applied himself to learning everything he could about the manufacture of marine steam engines. Roach also made a habit of saving money for the future. This provided him with an opportunity to purchase the Etna Iron Works in 1852 for $8,000. After its first year of operation, Roach's business showed a modest $1,000 profit. Over the next few years, the enterprise employed forty people and continued to expand.

By 1861, America could boast the world's largest merchant marine fleet, due primarily to new steam-operating vessels. Recognizing the potential, Roach converted his plant to the manufacture of marine steam engines. At its peak, the Etna Iron Works employed two thousand people. By the end of the Civil War in 1865, Roach had amassed $30,000 and emerged as a major force in the industry.

Following the war, Roach bought out most of his competitors, including the Morgan Iron Works. Established by Charles Morgan, the firm was then the foremost manufacturer of marine engines. In 1871, Roach added to his burgeoning empire by purchasing the well-equipped shipyard of Reaney, Son & Archbold in Chester, Pennsylvania. With its ideal river frontage of about a quarter mile, Roach renamed the yard the Delaware River Iron Ship Building & Engine Works. To support its operations, he established a string of other companies in Chester, rising quickly as the nation's leading iron shipbuilder.

Universally Popular

Shortly after opening his Chester shipyard, Roach began a long collaboration with Pacific Mail Steamship Company. Initially, he received a large contract for the construction of several modern iron-hulled steamships to replace the firm's aging fleet of wooden-hulled vessels. Later, Roach was commissioned to build the *San Juan*. Although other sister ships were larger, at 2,076 gross tons, a length of 283 feet and a beam of 37 feet, the *San Juan* was one of the finest in company's fleet.

With California's gold rush, newly developed steamships were demonstrating their worth. The vessels endured long voyages with better speed and greater regularity than sailing ships. The Pacific Mail Steamship Company was chartered during this period, offering the quickest travel and communication alternative to eager adventurers bound for "the land of golden opportunity."

The Isthmus of Panama became an important route between the eastern United States and California. Many prospectors sailed from Atlantic ports; crossed the Isthmus by wagon, on mules and on foot; and then took another ship for California. The Panama route shortened the voyage between New York and San Francisco to fewer than six thousand miles.

Previously, ships making the trip traveled around Cape Horn at the tip of South America. It was a challenging distance of nearly fifteen thousand miles. With violent storms posing a constant threat, the journey was not for the faint-hearted. "The gales at the Cape produce long, fierce blasts, bearing down on the sea and ship for hours," one traveler exclaimed. "Their effect is to produce long, huge swells, over which the ship mounts with a roll, then plunges into an abyss again as if never to rise."

The late 1860s were marked by great expansion of the Pacific Mail fleet. During the Civil War, the importance of the firm's service was noteworthy, forming the chief means of communication between the eastern and western areas of the embattled Union. Passenger travel west was heavy, and after the Civil War, an increased amount of freight was sent by way of Panama. The fleet enjoyed a reputation as "the most universally popular steamship line in the world."

Through the 1880s and 1890s, Pacific Mail began offering trans-Pacific services while developing its coastal operations. A dozen vessels, including the *San Juan*, were built and purchased for the San Francisco to Panama route. In 1920, Pacific Mail attained its greatest size, with forty-six steamers operating under its house flag.

The *San Juan*, and the rest of Pacific Mail's coastal fleet, was sold to W.R. Grace and Company in June 1925. By that time, Grace held controlling interest in the successful enterprise. He sold the house flag, good will and trade name of Pacific Mail to the Dollar Company, a popular worldwide shipping line, the following year. In 1927, the *San Juan* was purchased by the Los Angeles–San Francisco Navigation Company's White Flyer Line.

The *San Juan* was placed into service plying a popular route between San Francisco and San Pedro. "Every Tuesday, Thursday, and Saturday, a number of discerning travelers satisfy themselves that the White Flyer Line

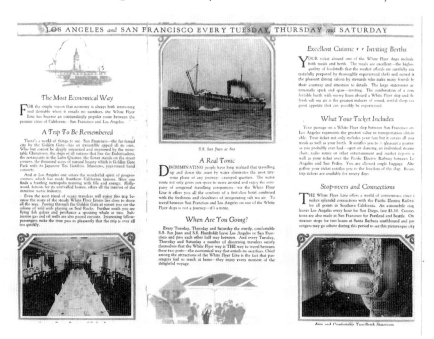

The *San Juan* sailed a popular route between San Francisco and San Pedro. A brochure promised "all the luxury of ocean travel." *White Flyer Line.*

is THE way to travel between these two ports," a brochure boasted. "It offers all the comforts of a first-class hotel combined with the freshness of invigorating sea air."

The fare was attractively priced at a mere eight to ten dollars per person. The journey was marketed as "the economical way that entails no sacrifice. One fare includes comfortable berth with snowy linen, excellent meals, open air dancing, promenade decks, individual steamer chair, radio music. All the luxury of ocean travel."

Memories of Only Tragedy

For most passengers, the trips were filled with anticipation and joy. Sadly, for other people, memories of a trip aboard the *San Juan* meant only tragedy. Traveling from San Francisco to San Pedro on August 29, 1929, the steamship collided with the *S.C.T. Dodd*, an oil tanker twice her size. The fatal mishap occurred near Pigeon Point just before midnight. The *San Juan* was sliced nearly in half and sank in minutes, plunging seventy-five men, women and children deep into the sea.

Paul Wagner, age twenty-three, was among them. Having secured a master's degree in physics from Stanford University, he was studying for a PhD. A teaching position awaited him at the California Institute of Technology. No doubt his future gave promise of a productive and successful academic life.

"My grandmother, Elsa, often talked about her younger brother, Paul, who was aboard the *San Juan* when it went down," Natalie Foster recalled. "She bought him a ticket to visit her in Los Angeles and always felt guilty about it. How sad she was, always crying."

Paul Wagner and his sister had survived a previous shipwreck. According to Foster, his family left Germany during World War I after losing their land and property. "My great-grandfather put them on a ship to Argentina to try to start life over. My grandmother was fourteen then, and Paul was quite a bit younger," she explained. "The ship caught fire and burned for days. It sank near the Canary Islands but everyone survived."

Paul's parents, Henry and Marie, reestablished themselves and worked diligently to educate their son and two daughters, Elsa and Anne Marie. Paul's death aboard the *San Juan* weighed heavily on his family. "The way Paul died, the way the accident happened, has always bothered me. He was physically fit and did gymnastics as a hobby," Natalie Foster reminisced. "If he'd had a chance, he might have saved himself."

Mrs. Willie Jasmine Snyder Brown, age twenty-nine, wrote a letter to her family before boarding the ship home. She revealed, "I'd really rather take the train, but the boat is cheaper. The children need shoes."

Married to Ulysses Simpson Brown, she had three young children between the ages of three and ten. The young family enjoyed playing the piano and singing. Her five-year-old daughter, Lorraine, was filled with foreboding about her mother traveling on the *San Juan*. She recalled having a terrible vision of a ship sinking as she gazed into a window pane. She kept murmuring, "Mama don't go. Mama don't go."

Lorraine grew up, graduated from high school and served in the Women's Air Corp

Mrs. Willie Jasmine Brown, a passenger who perished aboard the *San Juan*, took the ship because it cost less than the train. *Lorraine Spinelli.*

(WAC) during World War II. She remained close to her sister, Alma, and her brother, Robert. Yet, years later, a melancholy lingered over the loss of her mother. "The day I learned about losing my mother was a very emotional day," she uttered with tears in her eyes. "I was very unhappy and cried for my mother. How do you replace a mother's death?"

Lorraine passed away in September 2008. According to her last wishes, her ashes were scattered in the waters surrounding Pigeon Point.

Also lost in the terrible collision was George Navarro, a teenage movie extra who appeared in films featuring Ronald Coleman and Victor McLaglen, and Marjorie Pifer, who saved her son, the only child to survive the wreck, by throwing him onto the deck of *S.C.T. Dodd* as the *San Juan* disappeared beneath the sea.

FOG OBSCURED WATERS

The horror of the catastrophe was graphically reflected in the wireless messages that flashed from the two colliding ships. Just before midnight, the only radio message sent from the *San Juan* was, "We are struck! SOS!"

A message from the Standard Oil tanker *S.C.T. Dodd* at 12:11 a.m. declared, "*San Juan* rapidly filled with water and sank in a few minutes. Now picking up passengers. Are as near *San Juan* as possible."

At Pigeon Point, head keeper John Nixon reported in his log that fog was so heavy it was impossible to see more than a few feet ahead. Nixon and assistant keeper Jesse Mygrants were concerned that oceangoing vessels may be in peril. Mygrants noted, "Blew fog horns throughout the night. Heavy banks of fog are hanging over the water, obscuring ships."

The murky mist hindered rescue efforts. One of the McCormick Steamship Company's lumber schooners, the *Munami*, was nearing Pigeon Point when the *San Juan*'s frantic SOS blazed across the wire. "As the *Munami* pierced through the fog to the scene, we found the *San Juan* sinking," one of its crew declared. "We drifted in the wreckage of the steamer for two hours, locating a handful of survivors."

Most of the passengers and crew aboard the *San Juan* were asleep below deck when the collision occurred, giving them little chance to save themselves. "I was in my stateroom when a shattering impact awakened me. The ship shivered violently, and a wave of green water swept in," survivor Margie Dansby relayed. "Getting on deck, I was swept overboard by the next wave. The water was rough, and the fog was so thick I couldn't see."

CALL AND POST, VOL. 126, NO. 44
THE CALL-BULLETIN, VOL. 146, NO. 44

SAN FRANCISCO, TUESDAY, SEPTEMBER 3, 1929

Night of Horror Being Unfolded at Hearing of Tragedy

Denying allegations of the crew of the S. C. T. Dodd, which rammed and sank the San Juan, with heavy loss of life, surviving members of the ill-fated liner gave their version of the night of horror today | *at the federal hearing. At left is George Haines, assistant steward; center, C. J. Tulee, first mate (San Juan), and Joseph P. Dolan, federal steamboat inspector, one of those conducting the hearing.*

First Officer Charles Tulee (center) narrowly survived the *San Juan*'s wreck. He provided a clear account of the deadly incident's aftermath. *From the* San Francisco Call.

First Officer Charles J. Tulee was also one of the few survivors. "I was in my room. The blowing of the fog whistle kept me awake," he recalled. When I heard the *San Juan* and a nearby steamer each blow three blasts, I ran on deck knowing that a collision might occur. I was on the main deck when the crash came. A minute and a half later my feet were in the water."

Although overwrought at the loss of the *San Juan*, Tulee provided a clear account of the deadly incident's aftermath. "I was not near the lifeboats and do not know whether any were lowered. I heard no signal to the crew to go to their stations," he revealed. "It all happened so suddenly. There was not more than ninety seconds from the crash to the sinking. There was no time to lower the boats or put on life preservers."

Numbed by his brush with death, Tulee recovered sufficiently to go back to sea as master of both sailing vessels and steamships. In 1942, as master of the schooner *Commodore*, Captain Tulee was bound from Port Angeles, Washington, to Durban, South Africa, with a load of redwood. During the 143-day voyage, he became ill and died.

His colorful career earned him the title of "Iron Man of the Sea." According to one biographer, "Capt. Tulee had faced death many times in howling gales and mountainous seas and always was the bravest man aboard his ship."

SENSATIONAL SCANDAL

Following the *San Juan*'s dreadful misfortune, a sensational scandal erupted. To charges that the *San Juan* was unseaworthy, officials responded, "*Titanic*, a new ship, sank almost immediately when she received a blow comparable to that received by the *San Juan*."

Others speculated that the *S.C.T. Dodd*, which was badly gashed but managed to stay afloat, pulled away from the *San Juan* too soon. They maintained that the tanker could have saved more lives by staying with the wreckage. Meanwhile, officers and crew of each vessel blamed the other for changing course and causing the accident.

Still others claimed that the *San Juan*'s crew made no effort to launch a lifeboat or save a single soul. "If there had been any passengers nearby, they would have gone ahead of me," the vessel's third assistant engineer, John McCarthy, responded. I was on the ladder when the crash came, just leaving the engine room. The lights went out and I went out on deck."

McCarthy found two members of the crew and together they attempted to free the lashings of a lifeboat. "A few persons were standing about, but before the boat was ready, the ship sank," he declared. "I went down with it and was in the water an hour, hanging onto wreckage, before I was pulled out."

Ultimately, responsibility was placed on the third officer of the tanker "for not following instructions and for not reducing speed before entering the fog bank" and on the captain of the *San Juan* for "running his vessel at full speed in the fog, and failing to maintain a proper lookout."

The *San Juan*'s regular skipper was Captain John J. Winkle. For this voyage, Captain Adolf Asplund had taken command. Although Asplund had retired three years prior, the ship's owners had asked him to substitute for Winkle, who was away on vacation. Born in Sweden, Asplund went to sea at the age of twelve and later commanded freighters for the U.S. Shipping Board.

Dubbed a "hoodoo" skipper because of his jinxed history, Asplund struggled to keep a good reputation afloat. On one occasion, his license was suspended for allowing his vessel to sail without a full complement of oilmen. After a collision with a launch in Oakland Creek caused one death, his license was suspended again. Later, upon running a steam schooner aground, he lost his ticket for a year. Any insight he could have offered about the *San Juan*'s collision was lost when he slipped into the sea with the ship.

Families and relatives of those who were lost aboard the *San Juan* flooded the District Court with lawsuits. In January 1932, a final decree fixing claimants damages was settled. Standard Oil, owner of the tanker, paid a total of just over $329,000 in death, personal injury, lost effects and lost cargo claims. Of that, awards for deaths amounted to about $144,000, or approximately $1,900 per person lost.

Ghostly Witness

For months after the collision, the beach at Pigeon Point was littered with debris from the *San Juan*. Steamer doors, boxes, deck rail parts, luggage, articles of clothing and fragments of wood shattered by the boiler explosion as the steamer sank, created a coastal wasteland. Even the *San Juan*'s deckhouse floated to the ocean's surface on November 14, 1929. The remnants bore ghostly witness to a mournful voyage.

CHAPTER 12

CHASING RUMRUNNERS AND SARDINE STRIKERS

CG-256, SEPTEMBER 25, 1933

T he U.S. Coast Guard patrol boat *CG-256* experienced the excitement of chasing rumrunners, as well as the more serene duty of keeping watch over the strikes of disgruntled sardine fishermen. Her brief career came to a halt on a sharp snag-toothed rock at Point Pinos on September 25, 1933.

PROHIBITION ERA

The practice of smuggling liquor is as old as the substance itself. In the 1500s, the British government operated revenue cutters to stop smugglers. Pirates created lucrative enterprises running rum to heavily taxed colonies. As early as 1600, nautical terms appeared to describe a state of inebriation, including "listing to starboard," "carrying too much sail" and "decks awash."

By far the most famous period of rumrunning occurred in the United States between 1920 and 1933. The passing of the Eighteenth Amendment prohibited the sale, possession and consumption of alcohol. It proved to be an extremely unpopular law. Reveling in an otherwise liberated era, many citizens enjoyed a good stiff drink now and again, even if it was illegal.

A quote by Eleanor Roosevelt captures the essence of the times: "Little by little it dawned upon me that this law was not making people drink any less, but it was making hypocrites and law breakers of a great number of people."

Technically, it was never illegal to drink during Prohibition. The Eighteenth Amendment and the Volstead Act, the legal measure that included the instructions for enforcing Prohibition, never barred the consumption of alcohol—just making it, selling it and shipping it for mass production. Private ownership and consumption of alcohol was not made illegal under federal law, but in some areas, local laws were quite strict.

The introduction of alcohol prohibition was a hotly debated issue. Prohibition supporters, called "drys," presented it as a victory for public morals and health. Anti-prohibitionists, known as "wets," criticized the alcohol ban as an intrusion of rural ideals on urban life. Prohibition also created a criminal underground, as well as an unprecedented flow of liquor from the sea.

"The Real McCoy"

The task of pursuing rumrunners was assigned to the U.S. Coast Guard, a small arm of the Treasury Department. When Prohibition began in 1920, the service was ill-equipped to cope with zealous lawbreakers. Thousands of miles of coast had to be patrolled by a fleet of less than one hundred ships and a meager workforce of four thousand. Some reports indicate that no more than 5 percent of the United States–bound liquor was stopped between 1920 and 1925.

The first few months of Prohibition were deceptively quiet along America's shores. One of the earliest official references to the growing illicit trade was in the Coast Guard's 1921 annual report. The Florida coast patrol was cited as "particularly vigilant, having made hundreds of trips to support Prohibition authorities and seize vessels."

A Florida boat builder and excursion boat captain named Bill McCoy, who became the self-styled "King of the Rum Runners," set the pattern for smuggling liquor by sea. He brought ships to the edge of the three-mile limit of U.S. jurisdiction and sold his wares to "contact boats" owned by local fishermen and small boat captains. McCoy was famous for never watering his booze and selling only top-of-the-line name brands. Reputedly, this was the origin of the phrase the "Real McCoy," meaning genuine and on the level.

During his career, McCoy made hundreds of thousands of dollars and personally delivered more than 700,000 cases of liquor to U.S. shores. In his autobiography, he explained what drew him into this illegal trade. "I went into rum running for the cash. There was money in the game, lots if you could keep it," he wrote. "Beyond that, there was all the kick of gambling

A Florida boat builder and excursion boat captain named Bill McCoy became the "King of the Rum Runners." *Mariners' Museum.*

and the thrill of sport. There was open sea and the boom of the wind against full sails, dawn coming out of the ocean and nights under rocking stars. These caught and held me most of all."

The three-mile limit became known as the Rum Line, and vessels waiting to receive illegal spirits were called "Rum Row." In 1924, the Rum Line was extended to a twelve-mile limit, making it more difficult for smaller and less seaworthy craft to travel the distance. With the run to shore longer, chances of detection increased. In a desperate attempt to avoid arrest, some rumrunners dumped their cargo, set the vessel on fire and abandoned ship.

Often, crews armed themselves against government ships and against other rumrunners. Some rum boats sank others to hijack precious cargo, rather than journey to Canada or Mexico to restock their liquid supplies. At night, even in fog, they often ran at high speeds and without lights. Many smashed into rocks, spilling their profits overboard.

Ironically, one thing that rumrunners seldom carried was rum. The name was a holdover from the rum smuggling of colonial days and from the habit of referring to all liquor as the "demon rum." Most of the cargo was whiskey bottled in Canada and Mexico by professional distillers.

After California voted to join other dry states, rumrunners flocked to its shores. Secluded coves along the coastline became ideal locations for their illegal operations. Newspapers of the era are filled with accounts of coastal prohibition squads searching for huge caches of smuggled liquor.

"Mosquito Fleet"

With its many landing spots, proximity of good roads and relatively sparse population, the coast was a perfect place for clandestine operations. Nicknamed the "Ghost Coast," a booming underground economy revived many small towns. In some places, tunnels led from beach caves to coastal buildings.

Known as the "mosquito fleet," rumrunning vessels were small, astonishingly fast and adept at quick shoreline "sting operations." Most were thirty to forty feet long, with virtually bare hulls and small engines. Surplus wartime water-cooled aircraft engines turning out two hundred to three hundred horsepower were easily found and adapted. Some carried machine guns and even armor plating. Many kept cans of used oil handy to pour on hot exhaust manifolds, in case a smoke screen was needed to escape patrol boats.

Although countless rumrunning operations were successful, others were not so lucky. In the early 1920s, the steam schooner *Gray's Harbor* had several brushes with the law between San Francisco and Pigeon Point. Once, forty-five quarts of illicit brew were confiscated by local authorities. One December, holiday spirits suffered a setback when twenty cases of whiskey were discovered hidden in the quarters of the captain and first mate.

"Now, it was perfectly legal for skippers to carry their usual gallon of whiskey on board for medicinal purposes," the captain admitted, "but the law put its foot down on shiploads of whiskey."

In 1924, the steamship *Ardenza* developed one of the Coastside's most infamous reputations. The ship was created by a well-respected marine firm in Scotland, Hawthorns & Company and financed and owned by the ambitious shipbuilding entrepreneur Thomas C. Steven. Steven always had lofty goals, but his overreaching business approaches and risky endeavors brought him to ruin.

Designed to be a general cargo ship, the *Ardenza* arrived off Half Moon Bay, a favorite port of debarkation for illegal imports. At the time, Half Moon Bay was described as "a sleepy town in San Mateo County within easy driving distance of San Francisco." With the *Ardenza* came twenty-five thousand cases of scotch.

For several weeks, the ship stayed outside the Rum Line, still three miles out then, unloading her cargo onto coastal boats under cover of darkness and fog. From there the *Ardenza* continued up to Vancouver, where she was seized for debt, sold to new owners and sent back to Scotland.

In 1925, the *Pilgrim* came to grief on the rocks near Pigeon Point. Operated by owners in Astoria, Oregon, the schooner carried a cargo of illegal brew valued at $10,000. Much to the chagrin of many thirsty souls, Coast Guard patrol boats reached the scene quickly and confiscated the spirits after the *Pilgrim* drifted from the rocks to a sandbar. Not a single drop of the contraband, consisting of 175 cases of whiskey and 100 barrels of beer, sloshed overboard.

Prohibition created an extraordinary flow of liquor furnished by rumrunners. This boat is loaded with hundreds of cases of illegal booze. *Mariners' Museum.*

The *Pilgrim*'s flustered two-man crew scattered hastily, having already transferred much of the cache to waiting automobiles. According to Coast Guard officials, the racketeers nearly drowned attempting to salvage the remaining goods. In this instance, local residents were left high and dry. The following day, Prohibition agents located a hidden store of spirits believed to be part of the *Pilgrim*'s cargo. Officials exclaimed, "There was a truckload of whiskey."

Many rumrunners at sea were fast and well armed. In December 1925, the Coast Guard began a chase that began in San Francisco and ended thirty miles down the coast in Half Moon Bay. Despite the Coast Guard firing more than twenty rounds from the vessel's bow gun during the pursuit, the rumrunner *Gaviota* attempted to elude authorities.

The skirmish ended when the crew of the outlaw vessel deliberately wrecked their boat. The smugglers then jumped into the surf, swam ashore and vanished into the night. Three hundred cases of liquor were taken from the scuttled craft, netting the government a cargo valued at more than $100,000.

Rum War

During 1925, Coast Guard personnel increased to more than ten thousand. Nicknamed "Carry Nation's Navy" after the hatchet-swinging temperance leader, Coast Guard vessels consisted of an assortment of cruising cutters, inshore patrol boats and harbor cutters. As the rum tide continued to rise in epidemic proportions, pressure built to develop a fleet designed to meet the growing problem.

The largest single element of the expansion was the construction of more than two hundred new patrol boats. Twenty-five of the ships were built on the West Coast. These sturdy seventy-five-foot vessels, known as "six-bitters," became the mainstay of the Rum War. The nickname came from the colloquial term of "six bits," meaning seventy-five cents.

Built at Alameda, California, by A.W. DeYoung, the *CG-256* entered the water in 1925 as one of the Coast Guard's new rum chasers. Designed for seventeen knots and a crew of eight, the patrol boat emphasized seaworthiness and endurance over speed. Intended for offshore work, the vessel picketed rum ships beyond the twelve-mile limit to prevent contact boats from obtaining their loads of liquor. She was armed with machine guns and a one-pound rapid-fire gun. Aiding a more aggressive stance toward rumrunners were new agreements with other maritime nations that allowed the Coast Guard to patrol twenty to thirty miles at sea.

The newly minted ship was nearly lost before her rum chasing days began. During an early morning run on January 9, 1925, the *CG-256* collided in dense fog with the ferry steamer *Cazadero* near San Francisco's Alcatraz Island. According to the patrol boat's skipper, G.H. Jacobsen, a member of his crew was thrown overboard by the impact. Following an anxiety-filled search of twenty minutes, he was sighted and picked up by a small boat from the *Cazadero*. "The fog was one of the heaviest that has visited the bay region in known history," a local newspaper reported. "The ferry suffered damage to one of her paddle wheels. The *CG-256* was damaged considerably but remained afloat."

Prohibition, along with rumrunning, ended in December 1933. Between 1925 and the close of Prohibition, the Coast Guard seized nearly five hundred rum ships. Enforcing the law under Prohibition was the largest law enforcement mission in the long and storied history of the Coast Guard. "The fight against liquor smuggling is one of the most complex naval operations ever executed," Rear Admiral Frederick C. Billard asserted. "The Coast Guard was given the task, and it did not discuss it or argue about it. It simply answered, 'Aye, Aye, Sir,' and sailed into the job."

Sardine Capital of the World

With the Prohibition era winding down, the *CG-256* was given other patrol duties. In September 1933, her assignment in Monterey was cited as "observation duty in connection with the strike of sardine fishermen." At the time, Monterey carried the reputation of the "sardine capital of the world."

Known for their vast offshore harvest of salmon and sardines, the waters off Monterey were, and still are, popular fishing grounds. Although a fisherman's luck was always precarious, fishing vessels called purse seiners resulted in a larger catch. Their nets, which operated much like the drawstrings of an old-fashioned purse, were heavier, more efficient and could snare more fish. Many fishermen offered up their own version of a prayer by muttering, "May the holes in your net be no larger than the fish in it."

Finding shoals of fish at night requires far more than fisherman's luck. On moonless nights, it took experience and skill to spot the "green flash"

Hoping to improve the economic depression they were experiencing, Monterey sardine fishermen went on strike in 1933. *From the* Monterey Herald.

of schooling sardines. And the arduous task of deploying an unwieldy net off a moving boat on the open sea in total darkness took teamwork and courage.

Traditionally, sardines, also called pilchard, were canned "wet from the sea" with little pre-processing. Because of this, they were dubbed "wetfish." Sardine fishermen, hauling their catch aboard using the huge purse seine nets, were drenched in a shower of seawater, giving the term a double meaning. The work was both soggy and cumbersome.

Sardines were offloaded into buckets five hundred pounds at a time and hoisted by cable to the canneries. The pilchard were measured and weighed and then sent to cutting sheds. In the early 1930s, the bucket and cable method was replaced by a system of floating wooden pens, or "hoppers," anchored safely out from Monterey Bay's dangerous reefs. Hoppers were connected to the canneries by large pipe-like underwater hoses, employing massive pumps to literally suck the sardines ashore for processing.

ECONOMIC DEPRESSION

Originally, the grueling work of preparing and packing sardine tins along Monterey's "Cannery Row" was almost exclusively done by women. Often before dawn, a chorus of cannery whistles, each with its own pitch and pattern, called workers to the lines and warehouses. Cutting, cooking and packing continued until that night's catch was canned, no matter how long it took.

Sardines were cut by hand, drained and dried on wooden slats or "flakes." Large flat metal baskets of flaked fish were drawn through long troughs of boiling peanut oil, drained again, packed into cans and hand-soldered closed. Labeling and boxing for warehousing and shipment completed the operation. These canning processes prevailed until World War I, when canneries were mechanized.

During the war, the sardine industry surged. Orders for non-perishable canned fish poured in from both civilian and military buyers. Cannery Row's wartime sardine production grew from 75,000 cases in 1915 to 1.4 million cases in 1918. Similarly, the price per case rose from $2.14 to $7.50. Eventually, Cannery Row housed more than twenty sardine processing plants.

The wartime bonanza was, of course, too good to last. The end of World War I, and its ensuing recession, saw a scramble for survival by the sardine factories along Cannery Row. Reduction of sardines into fertilizer and fish meal, once a profitable sideline to canning, became a separate and dominant industry.

During the 1930s, most people in the sardine industry, as well as the rest of the country, were facing an economic depression. Many factories began laying off their workers. Unions began to organize in the commercial fishing and canning industries. However, wildcat strikes occurred often. Generally, they took the form of "tie-ups" because fishermen left their boats tied to the docks until a settlement was reached. During September and October 1933, hundreds of fishermen went on strike. They wanted eight dollars per ton rather than the six dollars per ton offered by the canning factories.

SENT HEAVENWARD

On routine watch along the fog-bound Monterey coast, the Coast Guard patrol boat *CG-256* hit a sharp rock off Point Pinos at midnight on September 25, 1933. Although the captain and crew attempted to free

The *CG-256* hit a sharp rock and sank in 1933 off Point Pinos. The crew survived, along with some of the ship's equipment. *Robert Schwemmer.*

the ship from the rocks, the engines lost power, and water sloshed through a hole in the hull. The skipper, Chief Boatswain's Mate M.E. Nichol, ordered his crew to the lifeboat.

In launching the lifeboat, the first mate's foot caught in a rope, slamming him against the side of the ship. Five shipmates leaped to his rescue. The slightly bruised and battered band landed safely on a rock near the beach. Several of the crew waded into the water to follow the shoreline to Point Pinos Lighthouse, while the skipper stood by his ship. "At the lighthouse, they were given hot coffee," one report said. "Their clothing was dried and some extra wraps provided."

Aiding the saturated sailors were keeper Peter C. Nelson and his wife, Ida. Nelson began his career as third assistant keeper at Point Sur in 1892. While stationed there, he married Ida Pate, a member of a well-known Big Sur family. The couple had two children, both of whom were born there.

The *CG-262* and the *C.G. McClellan* were sent from San Francisco to assist in salvaging the *CG-256*'s light cannon, machine guns, rifles, searchlight and assorted instruments. Crowds lined the shoreline, perched on points of rock. They watched breathlessly as the salvaging crew ran lines out to the pinioned vessel in an attempt to board it.

"When they got the lines on her and started ashore in the dory in heavy seas that crashed over and around them, the women on the beach let out scream after scream," the *Monterey Trader* exclaimed. "The dory would go straight down over the first line of breakers, then the second line would hit and everybody thought they were gone."

The salvaging crew survived, finished their work and abandoned the little patrol boat. According to one report, "All that remained of the *CG-256* was sent heavenward in the sparks of a funeral pyre."

CHAPTER 13

FALLING FROM GRACE

USS *MACON*, FEBRUARY 12, 1935

The most renowned wreck at Point Sur wasn't a sailing ship—it was an enormous airship. The mighty USS *Macon* fell from the heavens on February 12, 1935. When the remains of the sky-ship were discovered decades later, it was akin to finding the lost *Titanic*.

LOOKING SKYWARD

Just as some have yearned to cross the sea, others have longed to conquer the sky. A few even tried to sprout wings. Ancient mythology tells of Icarus, who wished so much to fly that he affixed wings of wax and flew toward the sun. Sadly, when the wings melted, he tumbled into the sea and perished.

Many others have attempted to soar through the heavens. Over the centuries, human flight has taken many forms. The earliest records date back to antiquity. In China, a primitive version of a hot-air balloon was developed; in Spain, a rudimentary glider was designed; and in Greece, a self-propelled flying device, called the *Pigeon*, was tested.

Italian inventor Leonardo da Vinci conducted the first definitive studies of flight in the 1480s. He created more than one hundred drawings illustrating his theories. Although his Ornithopter flying machine was never constructed, the design demonstrated how human flight could be achieved. "When once you have tasted flight," he predicted, "you will forever walk the earth with your eyes turned skyward, for there you have been, and there you will always long to return."

Airships were pioneered by the French in the 1780s. Brothers Joseph Michel and Jacques Etienne Montgolfier invented the first hot-air balloon. Using smoke from a fire, they blew hot air into a silk bag that was attached to a basket. The hot air rose, allowing the balloon to become lighter than air. Passengers aboard the device's inaugural voyage included a rooster, a sheep and a duck. A subsequent manned flight proved equally successful.

That same year, Jean Baptiste Marie Meusnier designed an elliptical balloon made of a two-layered bag. Soon after, Jean-Pierre Blanchard crossed the English Channel in a balloon equipped with flapping wings for propulsion and a birdlike tail for steerage. In the early 1850s, Pierre Jullien built and demonstrated a streamlined model airship at the Paris Hippodrome. The idea captured the interest of Henri Giffard, who built and flew the first full-size airship. Similar vessels became known as "dirigibles," from the French word meaning "steerable."

GIANT SKY-SHIPS

Throughout the 1800s, inventors continued experimenting with better ways to build and propel dirigibles. The first rigid airship, one that retained its shape from an internal structural framework, was flown in the 1890s. Designed by David Schwartz, it lifted off successfully in a tethered test in Berlin, Germany. Unfortunately, the propeller belts broke, the pilot lost control and the airship crashed. Following the accident, Count Ferdinand Graf von Zeppelin paid Schwartz's wife fifteen thousand marks for information about the airship. Zeppelin went on to found the Zeppelin Airship Company and produce the most well-known dirigibles of the time.

After they were used with varying degrees of success during World War I, fascination with dirigibles continued to gain momentum. "These giant sky-ships were the largest man-made objects of their time," marine archaeologist Bruce G. Terrell observed, "and their stately silence as they drifted overhead must have made them awesome to behold."

Following the war, limitations were placed on surface ship construction. However, American naval strategists believed that the possibility of enemy attack against U.S. possessions, such as the Panama Canal or Hawaiian Islands, still existed. Many thought that fast-moving airships could overcome maritime deficiencies and provide quick and effective defense.

The first American-built rigid airship was the USS *Shenandoah*, christened in 1923. Although she was intended primarily for naval purposes, it was also

Three men survived the crash of the USS *Akron* in 1931. Lieutenant Commander Herbert Wiley (center) went on to command the USS *Macon*. *U.S. Navy.*

expected that she would serve as an experimental prototype for commercial airships, of which great things were then anticipated. On September 23, 1925, she was ripped apart in a tornado near Cambridge, Ohio. Twenty-nine officers and crew survived, while fourteen others perished.

A larger dirigible, named the USS *Akron*, was constructed in 1931. She, too, came to a harsh end. On April 4, 1933, she crashed into the sea off the New Jersey coast during a violent thunderstorm. "Our first indication of being near the center of the storm was when the ship shuddered by the water. We couldn't see it for the fog," Lieutenant Commander Herbert V. Wiley stated. "The order was given to stand by for a crash. The ship hit within thirty seconds, and we were all catapulted into the water."

The dirigible sank rapidly, taking seventy-three men, including Rear Admiral William A. Moffett, chief of naval aeronautics and a champion of rigid airships, into the sea. Along with Lieutenant Commander Wiley, only two other members of the *Akron*'s crew survived: aviation metalsmith Moody E. Erwin and Chief Boatswain's Mate Richard E. Deal. Wiley was to have yet another date with destiny.

"MONARCH OF THE SKIES"

An improved airship, the USS *Macon*, was assembled at the Goodyear Airdock in Akron, Ohio. Hailed as the "Monarch of the Skies," she was christened on March 11, 1933, and based in California at the newly renamed Moffett Field. After a seventy-hour flight from Lakehurst, New Jersey, she settled into her new quarters. On October 13, the *San Francisco Chronicle* declared, "Mistress of the nation's sky fleet, the great silvery dirigible arrived with queenly majesty. While 30,000 people cheered, she occupied the five million-dollar home that Uncle Sam's Navy had prepared for her."

Formerly called the Sunnyvale Naval Air Station, the base had been renamed recently in honor of Rear Admiral William A. Moffett, who was lost in the *Akron* disaster. Located forty miles south of San Francisco, the field still contains the surprisingly modern-appearing facilities that housed the grand *Macon*. The immense hangar graphically illustrates the size of the gargantuan dirigible that nestled inside. Stretching 785 feet, the *Macon* required an area larger than two football fields in which to be secured. Placed on end, she would have towered as high as a seventy-eight-story skyscraper. In fact, the famed ocean liner *Titanic* could have fit in the hangar with room to spare.

From the outside, the *Macon* looked and functioned much like a helium-filled balloon. On the inside, the ship was an open cavern of girders, cables and catwalks, with men scrambling about like ants. The crew usually numbered between seventy-five and one hundred, although she was capable of carrying more. She was powered by eight twelve-cylinder, five-hundred-horsepower Maybach reversible motors. Those moved the huge ship forward and back as well as up and down. The behemoth had a nautical range of more than seven thousand miles and was able to stay aloft for more than 150 hours. In addition, she held 6.5 million cubic feet of helium gas and traveled at a top speed of 75.6 knots.

"The *Macon* was unquestionably the most beautiful dirigible yet designed, and uniquely suited for ocean reconnaissance," one admirer wrote. "She was twice as fast as the swiftest sea-going cruiser and had ten times the range of the longest flying fixed-wing aircraft."

Perhaps most spectacular of all, the massive *Macon* carried four double-winged Curtiss Sparrowhawks inside its cavernous hull. Utilized as scout planes, they were raised and lowered by means of a mechanized "trapeze." The planes were also used for defense purposes, since *Macon*'s sole armament was a machine gun mounted in an observation deck on the top of its hull, often referred to as "the nest."

The dirigible USS *Macon* was constructed in 1933. This ethereal photo by *National Geographic* illustrates the airship's immensity. *Monterey Bay National Marine Sanctuary.*

High-wire acts were nothing compared to the feats Sparrowhawk pilots performed. Each plane was released from the *Macon* from a hooking device, known as the trap, mounted to its top wing and attached to a cross-bar called the trapeze. For launching, the plane's hook was engaged onto the trapeze while inside the *Macon*'s hangar bay. Then the trapeze was lowered clear of the hull into the airship's slipstream. With the engine running, the Sparrowhawk disengaged the hook and fell away from the dirigible. For recovery, the plane would fly up underneath the *Macon*, moving slightly faster than the airship, and in a tricky maneuver hook onto the trapeze.

This hook and anchor system was dubbed by crews as the "flying trapeze." Hence, the logo on their now famous patch was based on the "man on the flying trapeze," an old reference to circus acrobats. "The big guy represented the air ship, and the little guy was the Sparrowhawk," former navy captain Gordon Wiley, Herbert Wiley's son, explained. "Once, a hook stuck. A Lieutenant Mayer climbed down with no parachute, and pounded on the hook with a wrench until it released. Then, woosh, the plane took off."

Eighteen months after the *Akron*'s demise, Herbert V. Wiley was assigned to command the *Macon*. With the loss of the *Shenandoah* and the *Akron* fresh in the public's mind, high hopes were pinned on the U.S. Navy's only remaining airship. The *Macon* was the final opportunity to prove that a military airship was viable as a source of long-range reconnaissance. Recognizing the significance of his assignment, Lieutenant Commander Wiley believed that only a dramatic display would demonstrate the value of Navy dirigibles.

When he discovered that President Franklin D. Roosevelt was vacationing aboard the USS *Houston* in 1934, Wiley seized the moment. With the *Houston* hundreds of miles out to sea, he dispatched the Sparrowhawks, which began dropping souvenir mail and newspapers onto the ship. "We gave those boys on the *Houston* a real thrill," former *Macon* pilot and Rear Admiral Harold B. Miller declared. "Our belly tanks looked like bombs, and some thought we were attacking the President."

Navy officials were quite displeased with the "surprise attack" and recommended disciplinary action. "They told me to show that the *Macon* could scout," Wiley remarked. "When I did, they wanted to court-martial me!" Luckily, President Roosevelt was duly impressed with the demonstration and interceded. Wiley remained on duty, and the *Macon* continued to fly.

COLLAPSED LIKE PAPER

Between 1933 and 1935, the *Macon* logged sixty-five successful flights involving 1,800 hours and ninety thousand nautical miles. She broke international speed records in April 1934, completing a flight from Moffett Field to Miami, Florida, in forty-eight hours. One newspaper exclaimed, "The *Macon* gave to the nation its greatest single demonstration of its efficacy as a war machine."

Around the same time, Wiley visited the Saint Francis Chapel at Mission Inn in Riverside, California. Dedicated as the International Shrine of Aviators, the extraordinary chapel still stands as a symbol of hope and protection for all who take to the air. Wiley placed hand-wrought copper wings on the "Famous Flyers' Wall." They were the first to represent the U.S. Navy. In later years, his wings would be surrounded by those of other aviation pioneers such as Amelia Earhart, James Doolittle, Jacqueline Cochran and John Glenn.

All went well until February 12, 1935. After completing maneuvers with the U.S. Navy's Pacific Fleet, the *Macon* proceeded north toward Moffett Field. Facing a sudden offshore drizzle, Lieutenant Commander Wiley remained composed. "The weather gave me no concern," he asserted. "We ran into two squalls during the trip and there was some wind, but the ship had gone through that sort of thing many times."

Nearing the Point Sur light station at dusk, a violent gust of wind struck the airship. Within minutes, the upper fin of the dirigible became twisted and crumpled, pulling loose the struts and girders. Helmsman William H. Clarke felt the rudder jolted from his hands. "Then," he exclaimed, "all hell broke loose."

Radio operator Ernest E. Daily sent an urgent message: "We have a casualty. SOS, falling. We will abandon ship as soon as we land in the water." Moments later, the mammoth *Macon* collapsed like paper, stern first into the sea.

Point Sur's head keeper, Thomas Henderson, witnessed the drama from his lighthouse perch. "I was watching the *Macon* through glasses," he reported. "When it was just about abreast of the Point, the fin seemed to go to pieces very suddenly."

"The fabric drifted back. Some of it caught in the rudder. I know there was a portion of the frame remaining, but I cannot say whether any of the frame was carried away," he continued. "The failure appeared to start at the forward end of the fin. The front part rose up, then crumpled back swiftly. I could see a hole at the top of the hull."

Having hurriedly carried out Lieutenant Commander Wiley's orders to don life jackets, the crew leaped into the water and scrambled toward rubber life rafts. "Capt. Wiley was in the control car. Most everybody stayed there until the end. But once the tail went into the water, there wasn't much more to do but look out for yourself," Clarke recalled. "We jumped into the water and swam out to a life raft, some on the inside and some on the outside."

Luckily, the Pacific Fleet's thirty-four-ship flotilla was still nearby and rushed to the scene, combing the waters for survivors. Admiral Joseph M. Reeves of the flagship USS *Pennsylvania* wired, "Right among the wreckage.

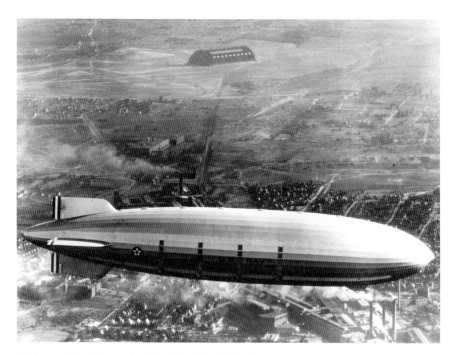

Christened the "Monarch of the Skies," the USS *Macon* soars over its gigantic hangar at Moffett Field, California. *Monterey History and Maritime Museum.*

Macon survivors in seven lifeboats located thirteen miles southeast of Point Sur. Rescuing same and continuing search."

Miraculously, eighty-one of the *Macon*'s crew found safety. Two others were lost. Mess steward Florentino Edquiba had run aft and disappeared. Radioman Ernest Daily panicked after losing his glasses, jumped out of the ship and drowned. Memorial services were held in the enormous, and now empty, hangar that had been the *Macon*'s home.

The *Macon*'s untimely end signaled the collapse of America's rigid airship program. Within days of the crash, Secretary of the Navy Claude Swanson said flatly, "I will oppose any attempt to build more giant dirigibles for the military."

REDISCOVERY

No effort was made to salvage the great silver dirigible. For decades, the *Macon* rested in a watery grave, 250 fathoms below the ocean's surface. Her four Sparrowhawks lay with her.

Marie Wiley (right) and Gordon Wiley (left) helped rediscover their father's airship. He's here with them and Herbert Jr. *Monterey History and Maritime Museum.*

In 1977, David Canepa snagged a piece of metal framework while fishing off Point Sur. The oddity was displayed at a local restaurant for years until Marie Wiley Ross happened by for a meal. "I recognized it immediately," she recalled. "I had walked among girders like that when I was a child. There was no question where it came from—my father's ship, the *Macon*."

Marie's brother, Gordon Wiley, told former Navy pilot Richard Sands of San Francisco, who represented the National Museum of Naval Aviation Foundation in Pensacola, Florida. Sands contacted David Packard, founder of the Monterey Bay Aquarium Research Institute (MBARI). His curiosity piqued, Packard referred the matter to colleague Chris Grech, who determined that it was a piece of duraluminium, almost certainly the *Macon*'s debris.

Fortunately, Canepa's logs were extremely accurate, and the relic's original location was identified. Armed with this information, MBARI developed a plan with the U.S. Navy to coordinate a dive in 1990. The Navy's three-man submersible vehicle, the *Sea Cliff*, rapidly pinpointed the wreckage.

"It became evident that they had truly reached the *Macon*'s last resting place when they informed us they had located the Sparrowhawk bi-planes. I could tell they were ecstatic," Grech acknowledged. "My own feelings tended more toward relief mixed with pride and gratitude toward the airship historians who had inspired others to undertake this daunting search."

Several artifacts were recovered, enabling investigators to generate interest in conducting additional surveys in 1990 and 1991. In 2005 and 2006, activities were renewed to obtain new scans documenting the *Macon*'s debris field more thoroughly. Oversight was provided by the Monterey Bay National Marine Sanctuary (MBNMS) and the National Oceanic and Atmospheric Administration (NOAA).

These organizations protect the waters, as well as the natural, cultural and historic resources surrounding the *Macon*. Through their dedicated efforts, a unique era in both aviation and maritime history has been recaptured and preserved. Appropriately, the site was listed in the National Register of Historic Places in January 2010.

HIGH FLIGHT

Like Icarus, the *Macon* once soared through the heavens and then fell from grace. Yet she remains the emblem of a time when new horizons beckoned and everything seemed possible.

One of aviation's best-known poems, "High Flight," captures the essence of the eternal desire to fly. Written by nineteen-year-old pilot John Gillespie Magee Jr. at the outbreak of World War II, it reads:

> *Oh! I have slipped the surly bonds of Earth*
> *And danced the skies on laughter-silvered wings;*
> *Sunward I've climbed, and joined the tumbling mirth*
> *of sun-split clouds,—and done a hundred things*
> *You have not dreamed of—wheeled and soared and swung*
> *High in the sunlit silence. Hov'ring there,*
> *I've chased the shouting wind along, and flung*
> *My eager craft through footless halls of air…*
>
> *Up, up the long, delirious, burning blue*
> *I've topped the wind-swept heights with easy grace*
> *Where never lark nor even eagle flew—*
> *And, while with silent lifting mind I've trod*
> *The high untrespassed sanctity of space,*
> *Put out my hand, and touched the face of God.*

CHAPTER 14

CRIMINAL STUPIDITY

BARC 1, MARCH 17, 1953

Perhaps the most unusual vessel to cross Pigeon Point's shores was the *BARC 1*. Under tow by a large U.S. Army tug, the experimental barge amphibious resupply cargo craft disappeared mysteriously on March 17, 1953. Bobbing helplessly amid the breakers were the bodies of three crew. It was the most tragic evidence of her untimely departure.

SWASHBUCKLING SCIENTIST

The *BARC 1* was designed by Dr. Thomas C. Poulter, a physicist and explorer. As a senior scientist, he participated in the Second Byrd Antarctic Expedition in 1934. He is credited with saving Rear Admiral Richard E. Byrd's life, plowing his way in a snow tractor to the advance base hut where Byrd lay ill with carbon monoxide poisoning.

Following the expedition, Poulter became associate director of the Armour Research Foundation in Chicago, Illinois, where he designed the Antarctic snow cruiser. A swashbuckler among scientists, Poulter capitalized on the excitement concerning Antarctic exploration by taking the vehicle on its first overland trip from Chicago to Boston and then to Philadelphia.

Few events were more colorful. The machine was driven first to Grant Park in Chicago's Loop to demonstrate its maneuverability to the public before starting for Boston over the highways. As the vehicle lumbered across each state, Highway Patrol stopped traffic all along the route. A

Dr. Thomas C. Poulter (left) participated with Rear Admiral Richard E. Byrd (right) in Byrd's 1934 Antarctic Expedition. *Library of Congress.*

special visit was made in New York so that blind children could "get a feel of the size of it."

In 1948, Poulter joined the Stanford Research Institute in Menlo Park, California, where he remained until his death at eighty-one in 1978. He was noted for "kindling the flame for scientific curiosity." During that period, his research ranged widely, from the dynamic phenomena of explosives and ballistics to the communication of marine animals. "I came to have an almost worshipful regard for Dr. Poulter's mechanical ingenuity, his intuitive use of physics and chemistry as a way of life," one of his students reminisced, "and his devotion to experimental research."

When the Army Transportation Research and Development Station at Fort Eustis, Virginia, inaugurated a feasibility study in August 1951 to create a large amphibious barge, Poulter was tapped to bring it to reality. The effort spawned a high-capacity amphibious craft able to perform over-the-beach resupply missions far more efficiently than previously possible.

BOXCAR TAKING TO SEA

The *BARC 1* was one of the new concepts pioneered during the 1950s to inject greater efficiency into the Army transportation system. A critical problem was delivering cargo in harbors lacking pier facilities. At remote islands or isolated supply stations, goods were handled at least twice before reaching a final destination. In the urgency of war, these delays were a serious disadvantage. The *BARC 1* promised to be the solution.

The first of four prototypes, the *BARC 1* was built by Pacific Car and Foundry Company of Seattle, Washington. In the 1950s, the firm was the leading builder of railway and industrial cars, including boxcars. The diversified enterprise also manufactured tractor winches, cranes and bulldozer equipment and fabricated steel for bridges, dams and factories.

The *BARC 1*'s dimensions were enough to dwarf any previous amphibian. The one-hundred-ton barge was sixty-one feet long by twenty-eight feet wide, with a height of nearly twenty feet. She carried six hundred gallons of fuel and a crew of two to six men. The cargo compartment was spacious enough to carry immense vehicles, including a thirty-four-ton Sherman tank and a thirty-ton crane, in one load. Across the front was a ramp that could be lowered for loading or unloading motorized vehicles and other heavy equipment.

Propulsion in the water was accomplished by a pair of forty-eight-inch-diameter propellers. On land, each of the four wheels was independently driven by its own 165-horsepower diesel engine and an automatic three-

Dr. Poulter capitalized on the excitement over Antarctic exploration by driving a huge snow cruiser on its first overland trip. *Linda Hall Library.*

speed transmission. The operating range with a normal sixty-ton payload was 75 miles in water and 150 miles on land. In an emergency, an additional forty tons could be carried.

Another of the *BARC 1*'s distinguishing features was her "crabbing" function. Both on land and on sea, she could move sideways in an indirect or diagonal manner. This meant that the vessel had excellent maneuverability and could adeptly avoid most obstacles.

The experimental *BARC 1* presented Poulter with a unique set of challenges. "I was given the job of testing it [for the Army Transportation Corps] for withstanding severe jolts that would be expected when coming in through heavy surf with a heavy load," he explained.

Initial tests were conducted at Fort Lawton, Washington, in the fall of 1952. The *BARC 1* was suspended on columns and jacked up to various heights. Then, the pins supporting the corners of the beams were filled with a small charge and exploded simultaneously. As the hefty craft plopped onto her tires, accelerometers calculated the force involved. Since the wheels were attached solidly to the body and lacked springs, it was essential that the tires were capable of absorbing the shock.

Other tests took place in the nearby waters of Puget Sound. "Looking somewhat like a boxcar taking to sea," one observer noted, the *BARC 1* paddled off and returned to shore in a slow arc. The world's largest amphibian crawled back on the beach, climbed small dunes without lurching and then rolled smoothly up a sandy hillside with a thirty-degree slope. Poulter declared proudly, "The *BARC 1* met all specifications."

A Beast

Developed to support a broad range of U.S. Army operations worldwide, the *BARC 1* was more than just a novelty. Over time, watercraft based on Poulter's prototype became essential in moving cargo from offshore supply vessels to beaches or inland transfer areas.

In June 1954, one officer and twenty-seven enlisted men formed a Barge Amphibious Resupply Cargo Platoon to train in off-shore operations along the coast of Northern France. The exercises resulted from the fear that the Soviet Union, which had recently acquired the nuclear bomb, might attack ports difficult to supply.

One barge undertook an initial mission in the Arctic in 1956, successfully carrying sixty tons of cargo from ship to shore. Four others were active in

1958 in Greenland delivering more than four thousand tons of cargo from supply ships to remote army bases supporting the Distant Early Warning (DEW) Line. The DEW Line was a radar system built across Alaska, Canada, Newfoundland, Labrador, the Baffin Islands and Greenland to protect the United States from Soviet attack. It was the largest Arctic construction and manning project undertaken up to that time.

During the Vietnam War, BARCs were used widely. Nearly every operation, whether on land or in water, was hazardous. Water operations were particularly dangerous due to adverse weather conditions, difficult tasks and enemy action. These mighty amphibians were the only craft in the U.S. Army inventory capable of landing on a beach through breaking surf, carrying enormous loads of equipment and supplies. "It was a beast, able to carry a medium sized locomotive," one veteran exclaimed. "It made an unforgettable sound."

Powerhouses though they were, the brawny barges had their disadvantages. On land, the driver had no vision from the control cabin located near the rear of the craft, relying instead on hand signals from a crew member on the bow. On earlier hulls, the control cabin was near the front, but raising and lowering of the loading ramp jarred the control panel badly.

The craft's greatest weakness was the air compressors. Located deep down in the engine room next to the marine gear, engineers often overlooked them

The *BARC 1*, first of four prototypes, was the only amphibious craft capable of landing on a beach through breaking surf. *U.S. Army Transport Museum.*

in their engine checks. Since the entire system depended on air pressure, serious mishaps could occur. In addition, the nine-foot tires tended to heat and swell to the bursting point, a common problem with amphibians. If one went flat, it took an hour to inflate. "Since the wheels on the BARC are larger," a crewman shrugged, "the problem is larger."

Although the exact number of *BARCs* built is unknown, at least fifty-four were once in operation. The last one was deactivated in 2001. In recent years, a few of the hardy barges have emerged for sale to the general public. Although, according to one salesman, "It's definitely a niche vehicle."

DIFFICULT TO SINK

The *BARC 1* raised as much curiosity in the early 1950s as today. When she was shipped from Puget Sound, Washington, to Monterey, California, inquisitive civilians took rides on the husky craft. "We cruised along at 10 to 15 miles per hour," reported one enthusiast. "It was like riding in a giant bathtub with wheels."

In her final evaluation tests, the *BARC 1* was side-launched into Monterey Bay from the deck of a tank landing ship. Confident of the seaworthiness of their craft, Captain Marshall W. Esslinger and one crewman rode the amphibian down the twenty-three-foot drop.

It was a rocky finale. On the final plunge, the hulking barge was almost completely submerged by water. Nonetheless, the *BARC 1* took the dunking without mishap and executed many successful beach landings, buffeting waves as high as fifteen feet.

"It would be a difficult vessel to sink," Dr. Poulter insisted. One side of the barge's inner structure could be flooded, the ramp could be open and a heavy load could weigh the craft down until the cargo deck was awash. Yet the *BARC 1* could still make it to shore, climb the beach on the power of two engines and roll to her destination at reduced speed.

When these tests were finished, the *BARC 1* was scheduled for towing to San Francisco. She was to sail under the Golden Gate Bridge on March 19, 1953, and proceed to the Presidio for a public demonstration. Even so, the giant amphibian would face one last challenge. On February 23, a howling sixty-mile-per-hour gale drove seven fishing vessels worth $500,000 from their moorings in Monterey Harbor.

Captain Esslinger promptly agreed to use the *BARC 1* in the salvage efforts. He and his crew worked around the clock to salvage the stranded fishing boats. "The roar of its engines could be heard throughout Monterey," local newspapers reported, "as it churned through the sand pushing stranded boats like a bulldozer or pulled at them from deep water like a tug. It was a miracle."

Among those rescued was the $100,000 purse seiner *Rosanna*. The eighty-foot vessel was the last of the stranded ships to be floated. Unhappily, just three days later, the *Rosanna* sank off Pigeon Point while under tow to San Francisco for repairs. Apparently, her seams opened, and she took on more water than the emergency pumps could handle.

WASHED UP ON THE BEACH

On March 17, 1953, Captain Esslinger insisted that the *BARC 1* depart at 1:30 p.m. rather than earlier, which would have taken advantage of the maximum number of daylight hours. Unluckily, as darkness, fog and rough seas set in, trouble began.

In water, the *BARC 1*'s maximum speed was 7.5 miles per hour. As the powerful Army tug gained momentum, the *BARC 1* was swamped by heavy waves and towed beneath the sea. The long stretch of cable and fog prevented visual communication between the two ships, and for some baffling reason, the *BARC 1* carried no radio.

In the murky darkness, the tug's captain saw nothing amiss until the cable parted. Although he contacted the Coast Guard to report the craft missing, it was too late. The *BARC 1* had disappeared, sinking in exactly the same spot as the *Rosanna*, the ship she had saved. Rescue units found Captain Esslinger and two crew floating lifelessly amid the frigid waves, still clad in their life jackets.

Onshore, James "Bud" Stevens of the U.S. Coast Guard was stationed at Pigeon Point. Bud arrived in November 1952 after serving at sea on several vessels. "It was different than being on a ship where we were always on the move," Bud explained. "We stood watch in shifts and did plenty of maintenance."

Coast Guardsman Bud Stevens served at Pigeon Point Lighthouse in 1953. He discovered *BARC*'s huge tires washed up on the beach. *Bud and Kay Stevens.*

A saving grace was that he could live in Coast Guard quarters with his wife, Kay. "We did laundry by starting a fire outside in a wood stove to heat water for the washing machine. There was no dryer so clothes were hung on a line extending down the hallway of the Victorian triplex," she said. "Since we lived right by the ocean, nothing ever dried fully. Even the car stayed damp. Bud had to wash it down with water and kerosene so it wouldn't rust."

Their first child, a daughter named Deborah, was born at the lighthouse. "We had a lot of good times with the other families who had children about the same age," Kay smiled. "At low tide, we'd go abalone hunting among the rocks."

Several days after the *BARC 1*'s sinking, something much more shocking was discovered. "The *BARC 1*'s tires washed up on the beach," Bud revealed. "They were immense, over nine feet. We couldn't get over how big they were. At the time, we didn't know that anyone had been hurt."

EXPERIMENTAL JOURNEY'S END

Local tugboat operators accused the U.S. Army of "criminal stupidity." Ultimately, the skippers of both vessels, and a series of errors, were blamed for sinking the experimental craft. "It began with the choice of an inexperienced tug captain," they contended. "He never should have towed as fast as he did,"

Retired Rear Admiral Edmond J. Moran led the U.S. Navy's tugboat fleet at Normandy, France, on D-Day during World War II. It was the largest amphibious military operation in history. As an acknowledged expert on tugboat operations, he added, "Then, Captain Esslinger fastened the towing bridles to the *BARC 1* near the waterline, where the crew could not release them in case of trouble."

The tugboat captain was dismissed from his duties. Three months later, the missing barge was raised from 220 feet of water, three miles off Pigeon Point. Buoyed to Oakland, where she was dismantled for investigation, the *BARC 1* eventually completed her experimental journey.

In addition to the tug's excessive speed in rough seas, several mechanical failures aboard the *BARC 1* contributed to the disaster. These included a partial power failure, a fouled port pump, a clogged starboard drain and a broken winch, which prevented closing the vessel's ramp. Nevertheless, other units were built and used around the world. The *BARC 1* had proven her worth.

LIST OF COASTSIDE CALIFORNIA SHIPWRECKS

Point Montara
(including Half Moon Bay)

Republic—October 5, 1851
Isabelita Hyne—January 8, 1856*
Elfin A. Kniper—January 10, 1862
Maggie Johnston—1863
Mary Martin—1863
Colorado—November 8, 1868
Alert—November 28, 1868
William Taber—1871
Aculeo—October 17, 1872
San Ramon—February 1, 1875
Rydal Hall—October 17, 1876*
Ada May—October 27, 1880
Alice Buck—September 26, 1881*
Argonaut—November 4, 1890
New York—March 13, 1898
Leelanaw—September 23, 1899
City of Florence—March 19, 1900
Roma—September 21, 1908
Nippon Maru—October 22, 1919
USS *DeLong*—December 1, 1921
Gray's Harbor—1922

Californian—January 10, 1932
Virginia—December 4, 1932
Jugo Slavia—November 10, 1940
YP-636—September 13, 1946

Pigeon Point (including Año Nuevo)

Mary Stuart—June 20, 1851
Carrier Pigeon—June 6, 1853
Sea Bird—June 9, 1853
Sir John Franklin—January 17, 1865*
Coya—November 24, 1866*
Hellespont—November 18, 1868*
J.W. Seaver—April 10, 1887*
San Vicente—December 20, 1887*
Colombia—July 14, 1896
Triton—April 18, 1911
Point Arena—August 9, 1913
Iolanda—October 14, 1923*
Pilgrim—May 22, 1925
San Juan—August 29, 1929*
Tamiahua—November 6, 1930
Western Spirit—February 2, 1932
Ohio No. 3—September 18, 1934
New Crivello—September 24, 1936
West Mahwah—July 9, 1937
Southland—September 26, 1944
BARC 1—March 17, 1953*

Santa Cruz

Active—October 26, 1876
Greenwood—July 10, 1907
USS *F-1*—October 11, 1912*
Palo Alto—1930 (beached as an amusement ship)
La Feliz—October 1, 1924
Crescent City—July 7, 1927

Point Pinos (including Monterey Bay)

Natalia—December 21, 1834*
Commodore Rogers—November 19, 1837
Star of the West—July 27, 1845
Rochelle—December 1, 1849
Julius Pringle—September 27, 1863*
Silver Cloud—September 24, 1878
Ivanhoe—September 20, 1891
Alexander Duncan—November 6, 1892
St. Paul—August 8, 1896
Northland—September 18, 1904
Gipsy—September 27, 1905
Celia—August 28, 1906
Bonita—November 12, 1907
Roderick Dhu—April 25, 1909
Flavel—December 14, 1923
Frank H. Buck—May 3, 1924
Ida May—August 29, 1930
Tamalpais—March 21, 1931
William H. Smith—February 23, 1933
Italia—March 2, 1933*
CG-256—September 25, 1933
J.B. Stetson—September 3, 1934
Aurora—January 18, 1935
New Crivello—September 18, 1936
YP-128—June 30, 1942

Point Sur

W.T. Wheaton—1854
Senator—April 1874
Falmouth—July 18, 1874
Ventura—April 20, 1875
Los Angeles—April 21, 1894*
Majestic—December 5, 1909
H-3—June 29, 1915
Catania—October 3, 1915

Shna Yak—July 21, 1916
Raymond—February 24, 1917
G.C. Lindauer—September 23, 1921
Thomas L. Wand—September 16, 1922
Babinda—March 4, 1923*
Ampullaria—October 21, 1925
Rhine Maru—March 28, 1930
Panama—April 9, 1930
S. Catania—April 13, 1930
USS *Chicago*—October 25, 1933*
Lupine—November 23, 1933*
USS *Macon*—February 12, 1935*
Frank Lawrence—March 24, 1946
Sparrows Point—October 24, 1947*
Howard Olson—May 14, 1956*

*=*Loss of Life*

BIBLIOGRAPHY

Chapter 1

Baker, W.A. *A Maritime History of Bath Maine*. Portland, ME: Anthoensen Press, 1973.

"Bath, Maine: A City of Ships." *Historical Ecology Atlas of New England* (2012).

"Capt. Bully Bob Waterman Founded Fairfield After Controversial Career at Sea." *Solano Times Herald*, January 17, 2018.

"Capt. Robert H. Waterman's Funeral." *Daily Alta California*, August 11, 1884.

"Captain Robert H. Waterman." *Morning Journal and Courier*, August 13, 1884.

"Carrier Pigeon." *Prices Current and Shipping List*, June 15, 1853.

"Carrier Pigeon." *Weekly Mirror* (Bath, Maine), January 1, 1853.

Clark, Arthur Hamilton. *The Clipper Ship Era, 1843–1869*. Riverside, CT: 7 C's Press, 1970.

"Death of Captain Bob Waterman." *Daily Alta California*, August 9, 1884.

"Disasters—Ship Carrier Pigeon." *New York Herald*, July 12, 1853.

"Even on Land Waterman a Mystery." *Solano History*, July 13, 2003.

"How Pigeon Point Got Its Name." *San Mateo Daily Journal*, July 6, 2020.

"Hush-Hush Tales of Captain Waterman." *Solano Historian*, May 1991.

"Insurance on the Lost Carrier Pigeon." *New York Herald*, July 12, 1853.

La Grange, Jacques, and Helen La Grange. *Clipper Ships of America and Great Britain, 1833–1869*. New York: G.P. Putnam's Sons, 1936.

"Loss of Clipper Ship Carrier Pigeon." *Weekly Mirror* (Bath, Maine), July 16, 1853.

"Loss of the Carrier Pigeon." *New York Daily Tribune*, July 12, 1853.

"Loss of the Clipper Ship Carrier Pigeon." *Sacramento Daily Union*, June 9, 1853.

"Loss of the Clipper Ship Carrier Pigeon." *San Francisco Herald*, June 8, 1853.

"Naming of Pigeon Point." *San Mateo County Times Gazette*, February 21, 1903.

Report of the Superintendent of the U.S. Coast Survey. "Sea Bird." May 16, 1854.

Rowe, William Hutchinson. *The Maritime History of Maine*. New York: W.W. Norton & Company, 1948.

Semones, JoAnn. *Shipwrecks, Scalawags and Scavengers*. Palo Alto, CA: Glencannon Press, 2007.

"The Shipwreck of the Carrier Pigeon." *Ballou's Monthly Magazine* (January–June 1871).

"Steamer Sea Bird Ashore." *Daily Alta California*, June 13, 1853.

"The Storied Waters of Pigeon Point." *La Peninsula* (Winter 2008).

Volo, Dorothy D., and James M. Volo. *Daily Life in the Age of Sail*. Westport, CT: Greenwood Press, 2002.

Whipple, A.B.C. *The Challenge*. New York: William Morrow & Company, 1987.

"Wreck of the Carrier Pigeon." *Daily Alta California*, June 8, 1853.

"Wreck of the Carrier Pigeon." *Daily Alta California*, June 10, 1853.

Chapter 2

"Aboard a Transatlantic Packet." *Ocean Navigator* (September/October 2002).

Año Nuevo State Park, Franklin Point Historic Shipwreck Cemetery Report. "Perils of a Leeward Shore," 2017.

Clark, Arthur Hamilton. *The Clipper Ship Era, 1843–1869*. Riverside, CT: 7 C's Press, 1970.

"Disastrous Shipwreck and Loss of Life." *Daily Alta California*, January 19, 1865.

"From San Francisco Loss of the Ship Sir John Franklin." *New York Times*, January 21, 1865.

La Grange, Jacques, and Helen La Grange. *Clipper Ships of America and Great Britain, 1833–1869*. New York: G.P. Putnam's Sons, 1936.

"Launched." *Baltimore Sun*, December 31, 1853.

"Liverpool Packets." *Baltimore Sun*, 1848.

"San Mateo's Graveyard of Sailing Ships." *San Mateo County Times*, September 30, 1972.

"Shipbuilding in Maryland." *William and Mary Scholar Works* (2001).

"Shipwreck." *San Mateo County Gazette*, January 21, 1865.

"Shipwreck and Loss of Life." *San Francisco Bulletin*, January 19, 1865.

Shipwreck Data Base. National Marine Sanctuary Program, National Oceanic and Atmospheric Administration.

"Sir John Franklin Lost." *Daily Alta California*, January 19, 1865.

U.S. Coast Guard. Record of Wreck Reports. National Archives and Records Administration.

Volo, Dorothy D., and James M. Volo. *Daily Life in the Age of Sail*. Westport, CT: Greenwood Press, 2002.

"Wrecked Ship Sir John Franklin." *San Francisco Evening Bulletin*, January 23, 1865.

"Wreck of the Ship Sir John Franklin." *Daily Alta California*, January 20, 1865.

"Wreck of the Sir John Franklin." *Daily Alta California*, January 24, 1865.

"Wreck of the Sir John Franklin." *San Mateo County Gazette*, February 11, 1865.

Chapter 3

"Along the Wharves." *Daily Alta California*, October 20, 1876.

"Ancient Anchor Retrieved." *Burlingame Advance-Star*, February 20, 1971.

"Bringing Rydal Hall History Back to Surface." *Half Moon Bay Review*, August 29, 2012.

"Cannon, Bell Recovered from Wrecked Vessel." *San Mateo County Times*, September 19, 1972.

Daunton, Martin, *Coal Metropolis: Cardiff*. Leicester, UK: Leicester University Press, 1977.

"Echoes from the Deep." *Retrospective* (August 2012).

"For Whom the Bell Tolls—96 Years Later." *San Francisco Examiner*, September 18, 1972.

Gonzales, John E. Interview with the author, February 4, 2009.

"John Koepf Obituary." *Half Moon Bay Review*, August 3, 2022.

Koepf, John. Interview with the author, March 12 and 14, 2012.

Neal, Frank. *Shipbuilding in the Northwest of England in the 19th Century*. St. John's, Newfoundland: International Maritime Economic History Association, 1992.

"Rear Admiral Casey Dead." *New York Times*, August 15, 1913.

Reilly, Mary A. "Santiago." Manuscript for *Methil Heritage*, 2007.

"Rydal Hall." *Daily Alta California*, October 19, 1876.

"Rydal Hall." *New York Marine Register*, November 1, 1876.

"Rydal Hall." *New York Marine Register*, October 25, 1876.

"San Francisco." *New York Marine Register*, November 1, 1876.

"Ship Ashore." *Times and Gazette*, October 21, 1876.

"Ship Lost When Captain Fooled by Fog." *Pacifica Tribune*, August 4, 1982.

"The Ship Rydal Hall." *Daily Alta California*, October 28, 1876.
"Shipwreck." *San Francisco Chronicle*, October 19, 1876.
"Wreck of the Rydal Hall." *Daily Alta California*, October 21, 1876.
"Wreck of the Rydal Hall." *San Francisco Chronicle*, October 20, 1876.
"Wreck of the Rydal Hall." *San Mateo Times*, October 2, 1971.
"Wreck of the Ship Rydal Hall." *London Guardian*, November 3, 1876.
"Wreck Vessel Sold." *San Francisco Chronicle*, October 21, 1876.

Chapter 4

"Alice Buck." *New York Marine Register*, October 5, 1881.
"Alice Buck." *New York Marine Register*, October 12, 1881.
"Alice Buck." *San Francisco Chronicle*, September 29, 1881.
Black, Frederick Frasier. *Searsport Sea Captains*. Penobscot, ME: Penobscot Marine Museum, 1960.
"A Brave Act." *San Francisco Daily Morning Call*, September 29, 1881.
Caldwell, Bill. *Rivers of Fortune: Where Maine Tides and Money Flowed*. Portland, ME: G. Gannett Publishing Company, 1983.
"Capt. Phineas Pendleton II: 79th Birthday Celebration." *Republican Journal*, September 6, 1883.
"Cargo of the Wrecked Vessel." *Daily Alta*, September 27, 1881.
"Death of Capt. Phineas Pendleton." *Bangor Daily Whig and Courier*, July 22, 1895.
Fairbanks, Ressa, and Marvin Fairbanks. Interview with the author, December 10, 2003.
Foote, H.S. *Pen Pictures from the Garden of the World*. Chicago: Lewis Publishing Company, 1888.
"Heroism to Be Rewarded." *Sacramento Daily Union*, October 1, 1881.
History and Commerce of New York. New York: American Publishing Company, 1891.
"Loss of the Alice Buck." *New York Times*, September 29, 1881.
"Marine Disasters." *Daily Alta*, September 28, 1881.
"A Midnight Wreck." *San Francisco Chronicle*, September 28, 1881.
"Mr. Gilman Cram's Tribute." *Bangor Daily Whig and Courier*, July 22, 1895.
"Notice to Dock Builders." *Daily Alta*, December 16, 1881.
"On the Rocks." *San Francisco Daily Morning Call*, September 28, 1881.
"Sailors Swept Away in the Wreck of Alice Buck." *Pacifica Tribune*, February 22, 1984.
"A Ship Totally Wrecked on the San Mateo Coast." *Daily Alta*, September 27, 1881.

"A Ship Totally Wrecked on the San Mateo Coast." *Sacramento Daily Union*, September 28, 1881.

"The Shipwreck Legends of Galen Wolf." *Mains'l Haul* (Fall 2006).

"A Signal Instance of Bravery." *San Francisco Daily Morning Call*, September 30, 1881.

Stickel, Barbara. "Coastal Exploration, Shipping and Shipwrecks." Historic Resources Report, October 7, 2012.

"The Survivors Account of the Wreck." *Daily Alta*, September 29, 1881.

"Taking the Sea." *Daily Tidings*, January 30, 2009.

"Trouble Among the Wreckers." *New York Times*, May 29, 1878.

"Wharf to Be Built." *Redwood City Tribune*, August 5, 1882.

Williamson, Joseph. *History of the City of Belfast, Maine*. Boston: Houghton Mifflin Company, 1913.

Wolf, Galen. "The Wreck." A story from Wolf's unpublished "Legends of the Coastland."

"Wreck of the American Ship Alice Buck." *Daily Alta*, September 28, 1881.

Chapter 5

"After the Wreck." *San Francisco Morning Call*, April 25, 1894.

"Blame for Lost Lives." *San Francisco Chronicle*, April 24, 1894.

"Blame for Lives Lost." *Santa Cruz Sentinel*, April 25, 1894.

"Blamed for Loss of the *Los Angeles*." *New York Times*, April 25, 1894.

Canney, Donald. "The Coast Guard and the Environment." Manuscript, 2001.

Coffin, George W. Correspondence from Office of Lighthouse Inspector, 12th District, San Francisco, California, April 17, 1883. California State Parks.

"The Cotton Fleet." *New York Times*, February 15, 1865.

"Her Last Trip." *San Francisco Morning Call*, April 23, 1894.

"Howell Scores the Captain." *San Francisco Morning Call*, May 11, 1894.

Le Boeuf, Burne, and Stephanie Kaza. *The Natural History of Año Nuevo*. Pacific Grove, CA: Boxwood Press, 1981.

"Leland at Fault." *San Francisco Morning Call*, May 15, 1894.

"Los Angeles." *Santa Cruz Sentinel*, April 24, 1894.

"Loss of the Steamer Los Angeles in 1894." *Lighthouse Quarterly* (Summer 2004).

"Mate Held Responsible for the Wreck." *San Francisco Morning Call*, April 24, 1894.

"Pacific Coast Steamer Wrecked." *New York Times*, April 23, 1894.

Reid, Whitelaw. *After the War: A Southern Tour*. New York: Moore, Wilstach & Baldwin, 1866.

Robinson, Ralph J. "Shipbuilding on the Patapsco." Manuscript, 1957.

"Sequels of the Wreck." *San Francisco Chronicle*, April 25, 1894.

"Settled on Her Side." *San Francisco Chronicle*, April 26, 1894.

"Steamer Los Angeles Wrecks Near Point Sur." *Keeper's Log* (Spring 2009).

"Struck a Rock." *Los Angeles Herald*, April 23, 1894.

"Sunk on a Rock." *Monterey Cypress*, April 28, 1894.

"Sunk on a Rock: Wreck of the Steamer Los Angeles." *San Francisco Chronicle*, April 23, 1894.

"Twin Shipwrecks at Point Sur." *What's Doing* (August 1947).

"Wreck of the Los Angeles." *Sacramento Record-Union*, April 25, 1894.

Chapter 6

"Anatomy of a Shipwreck." *La Peninsula* (March 1990).

"Captain Reed Exonerated." *San Francisco Call*, February 7, 1895.

"Climax of the Unlucky Career of the New York." *San Francisco Call*, March 15, 1898.

"Custom-House in a Rude Shanty." Unknown source, March 26, 1898.

Dillon, Richard H. *Shanghaiing Days*. New York: Coward-McCann, 1961.

Druett, Joan, *Hen Frigates*. New York: Simon & Schuster, 1999.

Durham, Dick. *Amazing Sailing Stories*. London: Fenhurst Books Limited, 2011.

"Fate of the Sailing Ship T.F. Oakes." *The Oregonian*, November 26, 1933.

Gowlland, Gladys M.O. *Master of the Moving Sea*. Flagstaff, AZ: J.F. Colton & Company, 1959.

"Ill-Fated Ship and Her Captain." *San Francisco Chronicle*, March 15, 1898.

"Ill-Fated Ship *New York* a Total Loss." *San Francisco Chronicle*, March 15, 1898.

Internal Revenue Service & Customs Journal. New York: W.C. & F.P. Publishers, 1889.

Johnson, Alfred S., Clarence A. Bickford, William W. Hudson and Nathaniel H. Dole. *Cyclopedic Review of Current History* 8, no. 4. Boston, MA: Current History Company, 1898.

"Last of the Famous Ship New York." *San Francisco Evening Bulletin*, March 14, 1898.

"Launch of the T.F. Oakes." *New York Times*, September 30, 1883.

"New York." *New York Marine Register*, March 16, 23 and 30, 1898.

"Oakes Towed In." *New York Times*, March 22, 1897.

Paine, Lincoln P. *Ships of the World*. New York: Houghton-Mifflin Company, 1997.

Peabody, Claire. *Singing Sails*. Caldwell, ID: Caxton Press, 1950.

———. "Then Three Times 'Round." *The Skipper* (March 1963).

"Perils of the Sea." *The Engineer* (January–December 1892).

"A Record of Events." *Brooklyn Daily Eagle Almanac* (March 1898).

"The Red Record." *Coast Seamen's Journal*, January 26, 1898.

"Reed's Crew Tells of the Voyage." *New York Journal*, April 13, 1897.

"Rich Cargo of the Wrecked New York." *San Francisco Chronicle*, March 15, 1898.

"She Stood at the Wheel as Sailors Died." *New York Journal*, March 22, 1897.

"Ship Captain Arrested." *Ann Arbor Argus*, April 2, 1897.

"Sinking in Her Bed of Soft Sand." *San Francisco Chronicle*, March 16, 1898.

"Tug Reliance Visits Wrecked Vessel." *San Francisco Chronicle*, March 15, 1898.

"What Is Lloyd's." *Ainslee Magazine* (August 1900).

Chapter 7

About Orkney. "William Leask." Biographical sketch, Scotland, date unknown.

"Another Stout Ship Lays Her Bones on Montara Reef." *San Francisco Chronicle*, March 21, 1900.

Bone, David W. *The Brassbounder*. Whitefish, MT: Kessinger Publishing, 1921.

"Captain Stone Testifies." *San Francisco Chronicle*, March 24, 1900.

"City of Florence." *London Board of Trade*, March 26, 1900.

"City of Florence." *Otago Witness*, April 17, 1877.

"City of Florence." *Santa Cruz Morning Sentinel*, March 23, 1900.

"City of Florence: Schooner Loaded with Nitrate Wrecked at Half Moon Bay." *Santa Cruz Morning Sentinel*, March 21, 1900.

"A Complete Wreck." *San Francisco Chronicle*, March 22, 1900.

"Court of Inquiry." *San Francisco Chronicle*, March 23, 1900.

Dana, James D. *Manual of Mineralogy*. New Haven, CT: H.H. Peck, 1868.

"Goes on the Rocks." *San Francisco Call*, March 21, 1900.

"The History of Clyde Shipbuilding." *Hub Pages*, June 2, 2022.

MacLehose, James. *Memoirs and Portraits of One Hundred Glasgow Men*. Glasgow, Scotland: MacLehose & Company, 1886.

Marwick, James D. *The River Clyde and the Harbour of Glasgow*. Glasgow, Scotland: Robert Anderson, 1898.

McCrorie, Ian. *Clyde Pleasure Steamers*. Greenock, Scotland: Orr, Pollock & Company Ltd., 1986.

"River Clyde." *Ordnance Gazetteer of Scotland*, 1882–85.

"Shipping Intelligence." *The Mercury*, May 4, 1872.

"Shipping Intelligence." *South Australian Register*, May 21, 1873.

"Shipwrecked Mariners." *Indianapolis Journal*, March 21, 1900.

"Shipwreck Information." *California State Lands Commission*, December 2018.

"Shipwrecks in Fair Weather." *San Francisco Chronicle*, March 22, 1900.

Chapter 8

"After Fifty Years at Sea, Capt. Rock Retires." *San Francisco Call*, September 8, 1898.

"An Ancient Mariner." *Taranaki Herald*, August 14, 1909.

"Arrived from London." *Sydney Morning Herald*, September 8, 1882.

"Becomes a Farmer." *Hawaii Herald*, October 6, 1898.

"Birds of Prey as Ocean Waifs." *The Auk*, April 1, 1901.

"British Ship Roderick Dhu Sold to an American Syndicate." *San Francisco Call*, February 13, 1896.

Cushing, John E. *Captain William Matson*. Whitefish, MT: Kessinger Publishing, 2006.

"Death of Capt. Boldchild." *Sydney Morning Herald*, August 2, 1909.

"Eruption at Krakatoa." Paper by Royal Society of Great Britain, January 13, 1884.

"Exports—Rhoderick Dhu." *Sydney Morning Herald*, January 23, 1882.

"First of Her Kind Afloat." *San Francisco Call*, November 27, 1900.

Gray, Captain Harry E. Oral interview by the San Francisco Maritime Museum, 1959–60.

"*Henry B. Hyde's* Fast Run." *New York Times*, January 1, 1895.

Johnson, Peter. *Memoirs of Captain Peter Johnson*. San Francisco, CA: Peter Johnson, 1938.

"Lost at Sea." *Liverpool Daily Post*, January 31, 1896.

McCandless, Michael H. *Well at Least We Tried: The Seaport of Redondo Beach, 1887 to 1912*. Redondo Beach, CA: Michael H. McCandless, 2000.

"Oil Barge Grounded on Sand Near Monterey Bay." *Los Angeles Herald*, April 27, 1909.

"Roderick Dhu of the Sugar Fleet Makes Good Run from Hilo." *San Francisco Call*, December 21, 1901.

"Roderick Dhu's Voyaging Is Over." *San Francisco Call*, April 29, 1909.

Roth, Lurline Matson. Oral history interview, University of Berkeley, 1980 and 1981.

"Schooner for Redondo Seriously Damaged." *Los Angeles Herald*, January 25, 1909.

"Seas Smash Roderick Dhu's Wheel Injuring Two Seamen." *San Francisco Call*, January 25, 1909.

"Shipping." *Auckland Evening Star*, August 13, 1909.

"Shipwreck." *What's Doing* (February 1947).

"Steamer Time Made by the Roderick Dhu." *San Francisco Call*, February 5, 1899.

"Story of Hawaii and Its Builders." *Honolulu Star-Bulletin*, 1925.

"Uncle Sam's Life-Savers at San Francisco." *Overland Monthly* (1911).

"Voyage of the Roderick Dhu Marred by Fatal Accident." *San Francisco Call*, January 11, 1896.

Chapter 9

"Cruiser Milwaukee Will Be Total Loss." *New York Times*, January 15, 1917.

"Diver Crew Praised for Bravery." *San Francisco Chronicle*, July 2, 1915.

"Evil Spirits Off the California Coast." *Monterey Peninsula Herald*, April 14, 1985.

"Five Hurt in Submarine Blast." *New York Times*, May 27, 1922.

"Growing Old Ungracefully: USS Milwaukee." *Lost Coast Outpost*, May 17, 2020.

"H-3 Escapes from Sur Rocks." *San Francisco Chronicle*, July 1, 1915.

"H-3 Is Refloated." *New York Times*, January 23, 1916.

"H-3 Reported Aground Off Point Sur." *New York Times*, June 30, 1915.

"Loss of the USS Milwaukee." *Underwater Archeological Study Report* (January 2020).

"Maritime Fiasco on the Northern California Coast." *California History* (Fall 1981).

"Milwaukee Ashore Trying to Save H-3." *New York Times*, January 14, 1917.

"Moran Ship Plant Sold." *New York Times*, March 18, 1906.

"Navy Beaches Sub, Cruiser on NorCal Coast." *Times Herald*, July 5, 2020.

"One Hundredth Anniversary of USS Milwaukee." *Times Standard*, January 7, 2017.

"Salvaging the Submarine H-3." *International Marine Engineering* (September 1917).

"Save 26 from H-3, Fast on West Coast." *New York Times*, December 15, 1916.

"The Valor of Inexperience." *U.S. Naval Institute Proceedings*, February 1967.

"U.S. Submarine Goes on Rocks Near Point Sur Lighthouse." *Monterey American*, June 30, 1915.

"U.S. Submarine H-3 Goes on the Rocks South of Monterey." *San Francisco Chronicle*, June 30, 1915.

"U.S. Submarine Is Reported on Rocks at Point Sur." *Monterey Daily Cypress*, June 30, 1915.

"Wreck of the Milwaukee." *North Coast Journal*, August 2, 2012.

Chapter 10

"Babinda Burns to Water's Edge." *Santa Cruz Evening Sentinel.*" March 5, 1923.

"Babinda Sinks." *San Francisco Chronicle*, March 5, 1923.

"Burning Steamer 15 Miles Out." *Santa Cruz Morning Sentinel*, March 4, 1923.

"Colima's Final Hour." *San Francisco Call*, August 15, 1895.

A Continuous Cyclopedia and Digest of Current Events. Information Annual. New York: Cumulative Digest Publishing, 1916.

"Crew Periled as Fire Takes Wooden Ship." *San Francisco Examiner*, March 4, 1923.

"Flames Claim Vessel Babinda Off Santa Cruz." *San Francisco Chronicle*, March 4, 1923.

"Four Sloan Ships Figure in Big Deal." *Washington Standard*, August 15, 1919.

"Lives Were Lost." *Santa Cruz Sentinel*, May 30, 1895.

"Motorship Babinda Destroyed by Fire off Santa Cruz." *Santa Cruz Evening News*, March 3, 1923.

"Motorship Is Burned Off This Port Today." *Monterey Peninsula Daily Herald*, March 3, 1923.

"Overloading Caused the Colima's Wreck." *San Francisco Call*, June 1, 1895.

"Patterson-McDonald Shipbuilding Company." *Pacific Ports Manual*, 1919.

San Francisco Bay Maritime History Series. Oral history of Thomas B. Crowley of the Crowley Maritime Corporation, 1973–75.

"Sea Swallows Burned Ship." *San Francisco Examiner*, March 3, 1923.

"Ship's Mascot Tries to Warn Crew of Peril." *San Francisco Chronicle*, March 4, 1923.

"Took to the Lifeboats." *New York Times*, May 30, 1895.

"Wreck of the Colima." *New York Times*, June 3, 1895.

Chapter 11

"Air Messages Tell Wreck Horrors." *San Francisco Call Bulletin*, August 30, 1929.

"Blunders Held Cause of Fatal Crash." *Burlingame Advance Star*, August 30, 1929.

"Captain Last Sighted Clinging to Bridge." *San Francisco Chronicle*, August 31, 1929.

"Career Earned Tulee Iron Man." Unidentified news clipping, April 28, 1943.

"Cowardice Seen in Ship Tragedy." *San Mateo Times*, August 31, 1929.

"Crashed Coast Ship Takes Tragic Toll." *Madera Daily Tribune*, August 30, 1929.

Foster, Natalie. Interview with the author, April 9, 2012.

Hartford, William J. *The Successful American*. New York: Press Biographical Company, 1899.

"Heavy Sea Fog Perils Ship, Say Lighthouse Men." *San Francisco Call Bulletin*, August 30, 1929.

"History of the Delaware River Shipyard." *Nautical Gazette*, May 8, 1920.

"John Roach's Life Ended." *New York Times*, January 11, 1887.

"Ocean Takes Heavy Toll of Life." *DeKalb Daily Chronicle*, August 30, 1929.

"Officers Face Inquiry." *San Francisco Chronicle*, September 1, 1929.

"Passenger Boat Struck by Oil Tanker." *Spokane Daily Chronicle*, August 30, 1929.

San Juan Shipwreck Trial. Statements to inspectors, August 31, 1929, to September 11, 1929. National Archives and Records, San Bruno, California.

San Juan Shipwreck Trial decision, October 16, 1929. National Archives and Records, San Bruno, California.

"Sea Disaster." *Brisbane Courier*, September 2, 1929.

"Ship Sank in Minutes." *San Francisco Call Bulletin*, September 3, 1929.

Spinelli, Lorraine. Interview with the author, July 3, 2001.

"Survivors Reach S.F." *San Mateo Times*, August 30, 1929.

Swann, Leonard Alexander, Jr. *John Roach, Maritime Entrepreneur*. Manchester, NH: Ayer Publishing, 1980.

Testimony taken at appeal of Robert Papenfuss, November 22, 1929. National Archives and Records, San Bruno, California.

"Three Face Trial in San Juan Wreck." *San Francisco Chronicle*, September 6, 1929.

Tulee, Roy. Interview with the author, March 28, 2013.

Chapter 12

"Alameda Wreck Inquiry Ended by Inspectors." *San Francisco Call*, October 12, 1905.

"All Are Sent Ashore Safely." *San Francisco Call*, October 1, 1905.

Allen, Everett S. *The Black Ships: Rumrunners of Prohibition*. Boston: Little, Brown and Company, 1979.

"Busting Smugglers and Breaking Codes." *Naval History Magazine* (February 2020).

Canney, Donald L. "Rum War: The U.S. Coast Guard and Prohibition." January 1998.

Canney, Donald. *U.S. Coast Guard and Revenue Cutters, 1790–1935*. Annapolis, MD: Naval Institute Press, 1995.

"Crew Missing as Boat Hits Island Rocks." *Redwood City Tribune*, January 1924.

Davis, Jessie Mygrants. Oral history of her life at Pigeon Point Lighthouse Station, 1987.

"Dry Agents Rush to Liquor Hunt." *Half Moon Bay Review*, June 6, 1925.

"Early Unionism in the Pacific Coast Fisheries." *Waterfront Workers History Project*, 2013.

"Fishermen Tie Up Sardine Packing on Coast." *Western Worker*, October 2, 1933.

Funderburg, J. Anne. *Rumrunners: Liquor Smugglers on American Coasts, 1920–1933*. Jefferson, NC: McFarland & Company, 2016.

"Heavily Laden Liquor Ship Is Captured." *Half Moon Bay Review*, June 20, 1925.

"Intelligence in the Rum War at Sea: 1920–1933." *U.S. Coast Guard*, January 2001.

Johnson, Robert Erwin. *Guardians of the Sea*. Annapolis, MD: Naval Institute Press, 1987.

Kemp, Michael Kenneth. *Cannery Row: The History of Old Ocean View Avenue*. Pacific Grove, CA: History Company, 1986.

"The Long Blue Line: Catching the Rum Runners." *U.S. Coast Guard*, November 19, 2021.

"One of the Heaviest Fogs." *Santa Cruz Sentinel*, January 9, 1925.

"Peter Nelson." *Monterey Peninsula Herald*, April 25, 1964.

"Point Pinos Light Keeper Will Retire." *Monterey Peninsula Herald*, December 22, 1938.

"Prohibition Turned Santa Cruz into a Smuggling Center." *San Jose Mercury News*, May 2, 1995.

"Rum Boat Cited Off County Coast." *Half Moon Bay Review*, June 27, 1925.

"Rum Runner on Rocks Today at Pigeon Point." *San Mateo Times*, May 22, 1925.

"Rum Ship on Rocks at Pigeon Point." *Redwood City Tribune*, May 22, 1925.

"Rum Ships Go on Rocks." *Half Moon Bay Review*, May 23, 1925.

"Sardine Industry Tied Up." *Western Worker*, October 9, 1933.

Severn, Bill. *The End of the Roaring Twenties*. New York: Julian Messner, 1969.

"Small Cutters and Patrol Boats." *U.S. Coast Guard*, July 23, 2014.

"Two Beached Liquor Boats Are Caught." *San Francisco Chronicle*, May 23, 1925.

"U.S. Cutter Cracks Up on the Rocks." *Monterey Trader*, September 25, 1933.

Willoughby, Malcolm. *Rum War at Sea*. Washington, D.C.: U.S. Government Printing Office, 1964.

Chapter 13

"Commander of Ill-Fated *Macon* Has Own Ideas About Disaster." *Santa Cruz Sentinel*, February 14, 1935.

"Dirigible *Macon* Sinks Off Point Sur." *Santa Cruz Sentinel*, February 13, 1935.

"Famous Flyers' Wall." *Army & Navy Register*, April 7, 1934.

"Fisherman's Records Aids in Locating USS *Macon*." *Lighthouse Quarterly* (Spring 2003).

"Giant Dirigible Macon Starts on Its First Cruise." *Santa Cruz Sentinel*, October 27, 1933.

"Into the Deep: Wreck and Rediscovery of America's Last Airship." *Noticias de Monterey* (Spring/Summer 2006).

"Lightkeeper Tells of Macon Crash." *Monterey Peninsula Herald*, February 16, 1935.

"Macon Broke Apart at Point of Old Trouble." *Monterey Peninsula Herald*, February 15, 1935.

"Macon Crashes Off Point Sur Light." *Monterey Peninsula Herald*, February 12, 1935.

"Macon Disaster at Sur Thrills Pack on Shore." *Monterey Trader*, February 15, 1935.

"Macon Probe to End Today." *Santa Cruz Sentinel*." February 21, 1935.

"Macon's Planes May Be Salvaged." *Monterey Peninsula Herald*, March 9, 1991.

Marshall, M. Ernest. *Rear Admiral Herbert V. Wiley*. Annapolis, MD: U.S. Naval Institute, 2019.

"Storm Didn't Cause Crash of Macon Says Commander." *Monterey Peninsula Herald*, February 14, 1935.

"Sunnyvale Will Be Converted to Landing Field." *Santa Cruz Sentinel*, February 22, 1935.

"Swanson Will Fight Further Dirigible Use." *Santa Cruz Sentinel*, February 21, 1935.

"Two Lost in Macon Wreck Honored Today." *Santa Cruz Sentinel*, February 17, 1935.

"USS Macon: Lost and Found." *National Geographic* (January 1992).

"USS Macon Turned Heads." *Daily News*, August 18, 2003.

"Wayback Machine." *San Francisco Chronicle*, October 26, 2008.

"Weak Construction of Macon's Fin Section Known." *Santa Cruz Sentinel*, February 16, 1935.

Chapter 14

Amphibious Lighter Operators Handbook. U.S. Army Technical Manual, January 1965.

"Army Amphib Salvaging Ships." *Monterey Peninsula Herald*, February 24, 1953.

"Army Board Reports on BARC Sinking." *Monterey Peninsula Herald*, June 11, 1953.

Army Transportation Corps. "Presenting the BARC." Research project briefing paper, 1952.

"BARC Invades Monterey." *Monterey Peninsula Herald*, February 13, 1953.

"Both Skippers Blamed for BARC Disaster." *Monterey Peninsula Herald*, April 22, 1953.

Defense Transportation Journal. "Preserving U.S. Army Transportation History" (April 1, 2011).

"Dr. T.C. Poulter to Speak." *Brown and White Journal*, October 11, 1935.

"Edmond J. Moran Is Dead at 98: Led Tug Fleet on D-Day." *New York Times*, July 17, 1993.

"Land and Sea Craft Sinks Off Coast." *San Mateo Times*, March 18, 1953.

"Looking Back After the 1953 Storm." *Monterey Herald*, September 12, 2021.

Moran Towing Company. "Our History." Brochure, 2023.

"New Type of Amphib Lost with Three Aboard." *San Francisco Chronicle*, March 18, 1953.

"$100,000 Bite Will Get You a BARC." *St. Petersburg Times*, December 5, 2003.

Poulter, Thomas Charles. *Over The Years.* College Park, MD: American Institute of Physics, 1978.

"Purse Seiner Sinks Under Tow to S.F." *Monterey Peninsula Herald*, February 26, 1953.

"Research for Industry." *SRI International*, March 3, 1953.

"Scientist of the Day." *Linda Hall Library News*, March 3, 2017.

Stevens, Bud, and Kay Stevens. Interview with the author, February 6, 2015.

"Thomas C. Poulter, 81, Polar Explorer." *New York Times*, June 17, 1978.

"Three Crewmen Lost as Giant BARC Sinks." *Monterey Peninsula Herald*, March 18, 1953.

U.S. Army Transportation Corps News. "One of Those Little Known Cold War Adventures" (2003).

ABOUT THE AUTHOR

Courtesy of Julie Barrow.

Author JoAnn Semones, PhD, boarded her first ship at age three. The voyage instilled in her a lifelong love of ships and sea sagas. JoAnn is best known for her engaging series about shipwrecks at lighthouses along the central California coast. Published by the Glencannon Press, they are *Shipwrecks, Scalawags and Scavengers*; *Whalers, Wharves and Warfare*; *Hard Luck Coast*; *Pirates, Pinnacles and Petticoats*; and *Sea of Troubles*. Volumes launched with and published by The History Press include *True Tales of California Coastside State Parks* and *Historic Shipwrecks of Coastside California*.

In this, her second book for The History Press, JoAnn presents a unique book about selected shipwrecks covering the California Coastside. Some wrecks had devastating losses of life, while some had innovative rescue operations or salvage solutions. From other wrecks, significant artifacts were recovered. One wreck site even became a cemetery that still exists today. Told here is the true and full story of each ship and shipwreck, their passengers, officers and crew.

JoAnn's stories have appeared in numerous national maritime and history publications. She has lectured widely and is featured in a video highlighting local maritime history that is part of a permanent exhibit entitled "Ships of the World" at the San Mateo County History Museum. She is also a consultant for California State Parks and for the Coastside State Parks Association. To learn more, visit her website at www.GullCottageBooks.com.